Beaten by Dinosaurs

Beaten by Dinosaurs

Sometimes, it just doesn't go to plan.

Richard Meston

First paperback edition December 2024

(Amazon) ISBN: 979-8-3026-1410-0

Independently published

Also by Richard Meston

Other books in the South West Coast Path Series:

Half the Path
Minehead to Penzance in 9 days. Via the pub.

Buckle Up
The five-year journey to the end of a 100-mile foot race.

Flippin' Hell!
The seed was sown 14 years ago... now it's time to run 84
miles across 185 million years of coastline.

Buckle Down
Hartland Quay to Minehead.
One hundred and ten miles, two feet, one path.

Running with Dinosaurs
The Jurassic Coast? Completed it, mate.

This one's for Oz.

Such a pleasure to watch on the drums and with a guitar.
Skilful, captivating, confident, focused and happy.
I'll take some credit for the music genes.

Outside of music, you're polite, kind and smart as well.
You get that from your mother.

CONTENTS

PREFACE

A pparently, a preface is supposed to *provide insight into the creation of a book, including the author's motivations and the journey of writing the book.* Having written 5 books so far, I thought it was about time I figured out what all these different sections are for. So, with that in mind, I hereby present my preface:

Well, it's a book about a running race.

If you hadn't already guessed that and were expecting an archaeological dissection of the Jurassic Coast UNESCO World Heritage site, you might want to do more than look at the title and/or the picture on the front of books from now on.

If you've read any of my other books, it's a safe bet you already know they're mostly about running races. The first one was about a walk (and I've got a couple more of those coming up soon, to spice up the repertoire!), but on the whole, they're about ultramarathons.

All of my previous works – or at least the ones about running – have included the part where I actually get to the finish line. I don't want to give anything away, but the title and the general synopsis may have already hinted at this one missing that rather important part of the race.

My original intention had been to write a short book – 20 or 30 pages at most – just to capture the experience of things not going quite as they should. After all, I've not only done this race before (successfully, I might add), but I've even written the book about it too (*Running with* Dinosaurs, if you haven't already read it). But as I was jotting down a few notes, my silly old brainbox started dragging memories out of the box I try to keep hidden in either a nook or a cranny (I'm not quite sure of the difference) somewhere between my limbic and parietal lobes. Like a parent trying to dissuade an overenthusiastic child, I tried to ignore the thoughts, but for some reason I couldn't stop writing them down, fleshing them out. I was enjoying the reminiscence, having a good laugh thinking back to some bits of the race, and getting a bit down in the dumps at others.

Part of the point of the exercise of writing these stories is for me to learn from my mistakes – to become better at ultramarathons which, for me, is much more about adjusting my mental approach than to doing more running… although I think that would help too. I'm beginning to get a little discouraged by just how many times I can make the same mistakes, and how little I seem to learn. Although, as I mentioned above, there are a lot of good times along the way, and I'm just starting to realise that maybe that's what it's all about…

And so, I invite you to delve into this book and enjoy the words on offer. While I encourage you to consume them in the order they're written, it's not a hard and fast rule. There are quite a lot of them which will take you on a journey from South Haven Point to somewhere further along the Jurassic Coast, a journey that – as you now definitely know – doesn't end quite as I had hoped.

1

Friday 21st June 2024, 22:20

As the last notes of *Break Stuff* faded and were replaced with clapping, cheering and screaming, the five members of *From Ashes* all took deep breaths and grinned at the crowd. It had been an excellent debut show at the Anvil Rock Bar in Bournemouth, and I'd been jammed up against a massive speaker stack with moulded earplugs protecting my hearing and a camera up to my eye, doing my best to avoid being bashed by too many happy revellers.

I'd had a beer at the beginning of the evening, and the music from the three bands that had performed that evening had been so much fun that I'd almost forgotten I had a race tomorrow.

Almost.

I glanced at my watch – half past ten. If I was just a spectator, I could have been out the door, on my way home and in bed just after 11 pm. To be honest, if I were just a spectator, I probably wouldn't have come along as it's not a brilliant idea to have a late night on my feet at a live music gig just before an ultramarathon. But I wasn't just here to watch. I was photographer, videographer, and more importantly, roadie for Oz, my 15-year-old son, who had stood up from behind the drum kit and was holding his sticks in the air, sweat

1

dripping off his face and a huge smile of enjoyment and relief plastered over his face.

When the crowd started dispersing, I got up on the stage and helped Oz dismantle the drum kit. Cymbals came off and went in bags, a surprising number of drums went into various cases, pedals into a case and sticks into packs. I left to get the car once the pack-up operation was mostly complete, and 10 minutes later, I was parked up out the back of the venue in front of a sign telling me just how much it was going to cost me if I got caught parking there.

At about half past eleven, I pulled up in front of my house with a car full of drums which I had no intention of emptying. Oz and the rest of the family were coming home in my wife's car, but I was a little ahead so that I could get in and get to bed. The unpacking would happen tomorrow, and my primary mission now was to have the dinner I'd forgotten to eat earlier through nervousness about preparation for the gig, and then get to bed. That dinner consisted of a tin of mackerel and a handful of Brazil nuts, then I headed to bed. I'd had one hell of a week.

Back in October 2022, I ran the North Coast 110-mile race. Hartland Quay to Minehead – from almost touching the Cornish border, through Devon and into Somerset over some significant lumps (including Great Hangman, the highest point on the whole of the South West Coast Path). At the time of the race, I worked for myself and had done so for a good few years before, and my usual preparation before an ultra was to have a few relaxing days beforehand, mostly sorting out admin tasks rather than wearing my poor little brain out with engineering thoughts.

But things were different for that North Coast race. I had been busy trying to get a software release ready, and as is typical in my world, this went up to the very last minute with me working early mornings, late evenings and rushing through preparation for my race on the morning I left for Minehead. High stress and not enough sleep resulted in a crushing low during the night, a mental exhaustion unlike any I'd felt during any other ultras. Luckily, it was midway between checkpoints, so I couldn't quit, and I managed to drag myself to the end of that race.

When I entered this Jurassic Coast race, I had a plan to have a really chilled week before the race. I've got a "proper job" now so have fixed start and end times, but that didn't matter – I could relax in the evenings, get early nights and make sure I was in tip-top mental shape (along, obviously, with being at my physical peak due to my perfect training regimen…)

And then everything went to shit.

First off, last November, my wife broke her ankle. Not ideal, as it turns out she does an awful lot around the house (yes, yes, I know that *now*, and I am now a lot better at doing the jobs I should always have always been doing!)

At the end of that month, I started a new job, my first change of employment since 2012. I love the new place I'm working at but having worked for myself on my own schedule for the last 12 years, the sudden change to fixed daily hours was a bit of a shock. I'm more the sort of person that has bursts of energy and does 6 months' work in a few weeks, then burns out and then watches Netflix for a week or two until I get bored and recover, then repeat it again. Sadly, that sort of thing doesn't go down well with normal employers, and I've had to adapt somewhat.

During the winter, I'd been training as much as I could towards my next race, the *Arc of Attrition* at the end of January, and things had been going… OK. Not great. For some reason, my resting heart rate had jumped up by about 10 beats per minute in December, and it hadn't gone down again. This coincided with running just feeling a bit harder than it should, along with an odd dizziness on runs that happened far more frequently than I would have liked.

Early in January, I went to see *Bring Me the Horizon* in Bournemouth with my youngest, Oz (the drummer), and we had an amazing time at a brilliant show – a great way to start the year!

The next day, everything fell apart.

My son had a car crash, ending up in hospital for 3 weeks. Thankfully, he was mostly OK once he'd recovered, but obviously I didn't run the Arc that year.

Everything had begun to settle down and we were a fair way along the road to a normal life again – my son much better and my wife just off crutches – and I decided everything that could go wrong *had* gone wrong, so I entered the Jurassic Coast 120 race with the plan that I could nail the full 120 miles which I hadn't managed to do the year before.

Next up, in March, was the 45-mile Green Man Ultra, a race I'd done 3 times before. You know that whole *everything that could go wrong had gone wrong* thing I mentioned… yeah, that was bollocks! The snow came down thick and fast on the drive to the race and I almost didn't make it to Bristol, the tail happy rear-wheel-drive car I was in slipping and sliding towards Bath, thankfully at a very quiet 5 am. I did make it, but a race that should have taken me less than 9 hours instead took over 10. I blamed the weather – the snow, the freezing cold, and having to wade through waist-high rivers almost ending up with hypothermia (I can't quite believe that actually happened mid-ultra!), but in reality, I just wasn't in good shape, despite the training I had been doing.

The final thing that went a bit awry – although in reality it may have been a blessing – was a change to the race itself. A fair few chunks of the South West Coast Path had decided to fall into the sea. Most of them didn't massively affect the race route other than the now missing steps to Houns Tout, and bits of the edge of Portland disappearing unexpectedly downwards with surprising regularity. The Houns Tout collapse added a couple of extra bonus miles, but at Portland there were enough diversions and potentially dangerous spots that Justin, Climb South West race director, made the wise decision to drop the 120-mile option, making the 105-mile run to Exmouth the longest race of the day.

While I totally understood the reasoning, I was a bit miffed to start with. This year was supposed to be my chance to right the wrongs of the previous year, hit Weymouth in tip-top shape and get the full 120-miles done with a smile on my face all the way. Or, more realistically, for me to crawl round Portland and then regret my life choices for the remaining hours, of which there would be a lot, eventually crawling over the finish line in the dark. In any case, the 120 miles was the target. But over the following few days I got my head around the change and decided the new plan should be to beat last years time – after all, you have to keep getting better, right?

My recent training plan for ultras has been to run 1,000 miles and 100,000ft of ascent during the 16 weeks prior to the race. With my new job, free time was at a premium, and I didn't fancy spending all my evening in the gym, so I went out once a week for about 8 weeks and ran at Lulworth – a spot about 30 miles into the Jurassic Coast race. I doubled up all the hills (i.e. run to the top, run back down, then run back up again before moving on), getting a brutal 4,000 feet of up-and-down in less than 9 miles. I had also planned to do a long run every weekend, and managed a few 15, 16 and 17 miles runs, over the preceding months, but that was it.

At the start of June, I ran 105 miles spread over 11 days just to cover the mileage. It was supposed to be an easy confidence boost but, on the whole, ended up being bloody hard work.

Ever the optimist, the super-detailed timing chart that I'd spent ages working on had my A-goal at just under 30 hours. With the extra detours due to bits of the South West Coast Path falling into the sea, that would be around 1 hour 20 minutes faster than last year! Once I realised that, even the optimistic side of my brain was suggesting that maybe I should calm down a bit.

Skip forward to June 17th, the week before the race, and everything had come along at the same time and my promised "easy week" went out the window completely.

Monday saw me and my two sons out at the O2 in Bournemouth jumping around to Royal Blood – a late night, a few beers (and a G&T in the queue – very civilised!), but one late night is fine, right?

The "Body Battery" on my watch had dragged its way up to a mere 30% by Wednesday, when I was out *again* in the evening at a college end-of-year music show in Bournemouth. It was another great evening, but I was yawning throughout, knowing I really should be at home tucked up in bed.

And then there was Friday – the *From Ashes* night that I started this chapter with. Already worn down from the rest of the week, I was lying in bed at 1am on Saturday morning, partly buzzing from the fun of the previous evening, and partly in despair about the fact that I was to set off on a 105-mile race in 7 hours, and far from being asleep, I wasn't even feeling tired.

2

Don't fall off the cliffs

Saturday 22nd June 2024, 05:30

I t took a moment for my eyes to unblur and for me to be able to see the writing on the screen of my watch. When the numbers swam into focus, I wished they hadn't.

Four hours and fifty minutes sleep. Poor quality.

What a superb start to the day. I scrolled through the "Morning Report" on my new watch to find my Training Readiness was Poor and my Heart Rate Variability had, for the first time in a few weeks, dropped into the Low category. I was beginning to regret having bought this watch as all it seemed to tell me was how ill-prepared I was for tackling a normal day, let alone an ultramarathon.

The alarm had issued its unwelcome beeps and buzzes on my wrist at 5:30 am, and at a little before six I had a cup of decaf coffee steaming away in the bathroom while liberally applying Squirrel's Nut Butter to various places on my body. I paid particular attention to my back, rubbing on a lot of the balm over every area I could reach in the hope that I might not end up with my skin being torn to pieces slowly over the course of a few hundred thousand steps like had happened for the last 4 or 5 ultras I'd used this Salomon vest for.

Fifteen minutes later, I was at the kitchen table, another cup of coffee (still decaffeinated) in hand as I contemplated the day ahead. I was awake – just about – but despite the slight zombie-like feeling you get after a late night and too-short sleep, I was really excited! It was race day, and I'd been working towards this and looking forward to it for months. Time for an *adventure!*

The band shenanigans the previous night at least meant I'd had to be organised, so pretty much everything was ready on Thursday and there wasn't a whole lot to do now. I refilled my water bottles, having left them filled the previous afternoon as a test and found that one had a leak – lucky I tested! Last thing left was to get my shoes on, which was usually more of a faff than you'd think.

My gaiters were already on, slid halfway up my shins straight after my calf guards went on, otherwise there was a fair chance I'd get my shoes on perfectly only to realised I'd forgotten the bloody gaiters! I contemplated spreading some Trench cream on my feet, but remembered I wasn't doing Cape Wrath or the Winter Spine and was unlikely to encounter too much in the way of foot-wetting terrain, so I slapped on a shiny new pair of Darn Tough Hiker socks and pulled on my newish (35 miles old) Altra Lone Peak 8's, which I really didn't like very much. The Lone Peak 7's were lovely shoes, much more padded than all the previous versions, still zero drop and really comfortable. I bought a pair of 8's as they were the latest and greatest, but it's like Altra forgot to add half the shoe and instead made a lightweight racer where they should have been producing a shoe for long distance comfort. The shoes would have to do as I certainly wasn't going to spend another hundred-and-something quid on a different pair, but I wasn't a big fan of these ones.

I got the gaiters clipped into the front lace of both shoes on the fourth attempt and that was me, done. From top to bottom, I had a lightweight baseball-style Buff cap, a merino t-shirt, Runderwear pants, compression shorts and some lightweight over-shorts, calf guards, gaiters, socks and shoes. If that isn't ready for a coast path adventure, I don't know what is!

The ferry to South Haven Point starts at 7am and runs every 20 minutes in the direction I wanted to go. The race start time this year was 8:15 am, a little later than last year, so although I was aiming for the first ferry, I wasn't panicking about missing it – which was a good thing, as Eva and I left home a few minutes later than intended.

Both the traffic and the traffic lights were kind, and we pulled up into a parking space a couple of minutes before 7. Before I knew it, I was up on the top deck of the ferry, nervously pacing in circles and waving bye to Eva while waiting to get sailing.

A little group of us wandered down the ramp after the 4-minute journey across the water, and we were chattering away while walking along the road towards the race meeting point. Someone said something behind me which I didn't catch, and I turned around.

"You don't recognise me, do you?" said a face which I didn't immediately recognise due to my prosopagnosia. I quickly scanned through the catalogue of facial features in my head, but actually this one was fairly obvious, if somewhat unexpected. Mr Stuart Webster – fresh off a finish at Cape Wrath Ultra – had come over from the Southampton area to say hello. What a lovely surprise!

We had a chat while walking along. He had a fairly hefty new pack which he was trying out in preparation for the Northern Spine race next year and had decided that hopping on a train from near Southampton to Poole, running 5 miles to the ferry and catching up with me at before my race would be a reasonable start to his run.

The race setup point was in the first car park just a short distance up from the ferry, and 10 minutes after arriving I'd passed kit check by showing off my waterproof jacket, long sleeved warm layer and head torch with spare battery. My number was duly pinned to my shorts, something I appear to be getting quite good at. I'd brought along a 2-litre water bottle to keep me hydrated while waiting, and so I was occasionally glugging from that while chatting with Stu, Justin (the race director) and saying hi to a few other people I knew.

Stu headed off back to the ferry just as the race brief started, during which Justin covered the usual things like don't fall off the cliffs (lots of paperwork), don't make too much noise at night (lots of grumpy people), you'll probably get lost (of course!), and have fun! It was a hot day, so Justin also told us he had planned an extra water stop somewhere around Swanage too, so we were to look out for that. And then he went and mentioned that I'd written a book about the race, at which point everyone looked over at me while I turned a not-so-subtle shade of plum through embarrassment, but it did

11

lead to quite a few conversations during the race (the book, that is – not my plum-coloured face).

Thirty-one runners nervously headed back down towards the ferry, the majority taking advantage of the toilet block enroute, and we all assembled on the sand near the South West Coast Path marker. With a few minutes to go, Justin took a couple of photos with his phone, making a valiant attempt to get us all to look enthusiastic, which actually just about worked!

At 8:15 am, under a blue sky peppered with fluffy white clouds which were doing their best to keep the sun at bay, we all set off along the beach on a 105-ish mile adventure towards Exmouth.

3

Bloody boiling!

This felt very familiar. I must have run from the ferry to Weymouth at least 20 times, with 3 of them as part of a race. I started the slow trudge on the soft sand towards the water, thinking to myself that the sand was actually quite firm today, and it was reasonably easy to run on. Nevertheless, I headed directly towards the water, and the group around me did the same unbid – it seemed we were a group of people that knew the best route around here, or at least trusted everyone else knew what they were doing.

When I reached the edge of the water, I expected there to be a nice flat section of recently washed sand to run along as had been my experience on every run I'd ever done along here. But today, for the first time, I hit the sea at the very highest point of the tide, and all that was left dry was an uncomfortably steep camber down to the water. So, it was good that I'd been thinking that the softer sand wasn't so bad, as that's what we were left with for the next few miles.

I kept to a moderately easy pace, settling into my own space in the long chain of runners that stretched out towards Old Harry in the distance. I did a quick head-to-toe assessment of how I felt and eventually concluded that all was good. I didn't feel amazing, but I very rarely do at the start of races. And I didn't feel awful. Everything absolutely standard for an ultramarathon, then.

My pace meant I was very slowly catching the couple of runners ahead, and after a few minutes I ended up next to Matt Dalton, who I met for the first time on the North Coast 110. We had a brief chat, after which I found myself just a little in front again, so I continued on that way. This was slightly worrying – Matt has been my benchmark, my target for a good race. If I could see him, even far in the distance, I was doing well. I'd never planned to be *ahead* of Matt, especially not this early on.

For long events I've taken to wearing padded fingerless gloves to stop the somewhat abrasive straps of my Black Diamond poles rubbing the skin off the space between my finger and thumb. I realised that I'd forgotten to put them on before the race and the lump where they were stuffed in my pack was becoming a bit uncomfortable against my side. I was also a bit concerned about losing them if they were to fall out (which has happened to me before), so I took the opportunity to distract myself from the running and wriggle them onto my hands. The other benefit of these – as well as stopping poles rubbing – is that if I were to fall over and instinctively put my hands out, which always seemed to be the case, the padded palms offered some protection. I'd got into the habit of falling over about every 6 months recently, and anything I could do to minimise the shredding of my palms that seemed to happen each time I splatted down was well worth doing.

The turning that took us off the beach came, and I walked quickly up the slope to Middle Beach car park. I felt I was moving faster than last year, which was good as my target was to be a few percent quicker overall – but it was coming at a cost. The race so far was feeling like quite hard work, and as I had over 100 miles to go, this wasn't how I was supposed to be feeling this early on.

The path continued past the Pig restaurant and hotel, the concrete behemoth of Fort Henry, and out onto the road past the Bankes Arms[1] pub before hitting the bottom of the hill which led up to Old Harry Rocks. The first section is quite steep – a good excuse for a walk – then it levels off on a gentle climb up to Foreland Point which marks the start of the Jurassic Coast World Heritage Site.

A check of my timing chart suggested I was a few minutes ahead of my target time, which, in turn, was a few minutes ahead of last year. I had a moment of relief – that meant the effort I was feeling was because I was going *too* fast – I could slow down and relax a bit, and that should make me feel a whole lot better.

But over the next few minutes, it dawned on me that in my calculation of where I was against the time on my chart, I'd misjudged the distance to Old Harry Rocks, forgetting just how long the climb was. As I finally broke out through the bushes and headed to the corner above the cliffs, I was pushing harder again just to try and hit the time I had for the turnaround above the cliffs. I was no more than 5 miles into

---

[1] Which I learnt yesterday, while watching Bill Bailey and Paul Merton wandering along the South West Coast Path, is named after the Bankes family who also owned Corfe Castle and the country estate of Kingston Lacy.

this race and was already thinking about ditching my target. If only I had, my race could have turned out very different.

The hill continued upward to the top of the ridge that, were I to turn inland, would take me along to Corfe Castle. This was a more significant climb than the one to Old Harry, during which I actually started to feel a bit better. A couple of racers that I'd been matching pace with went on ahead, but my rapid walking pace meant I overtook two more, and not wanting to be caught again, I kept up what felt like a fast but reasonably sustainable effort to the top.

I passed a gate near the top of the hill, one which you can often make a mistake at by going through and heading along towards Corfe instead of down to Swanage, but today the route seemed very obviously *not* through the gate, and I wondered how anyone could really make a mistake here. I was feeling good, not just about not cocking up the route, but also that I'd got to the top of the hill so easily and was beginning to feel a bit better. Something confused me though... I couldn't understand why – being at the *top* of the hill – I was still going up.

This continued for a while longer, until I met another gate which I opened to head through without giving it a second thought. A sudden realisation hit me – *this* was the confusing gate, that other one hadn't been anywhere near the top of the hill. I replaced the gate back in its latch and instead took the overgrown path to the left, telling the guy behind that this was, in fact, the correct route. He was moving faster than me, so I let him by as I knew there was a section of narrow trail coming up where passing would be difficult.

Having now almost reached the real top of the hill, I was feeling considerably more puffed out, and my legs were surprisingly achy. My quads in particular felt like I'd run a considerable distance within the last couple of days, which was odd because I'd deliberately done very little running over the preceding week.

The final section of the hill continued upwards on a gravelly path that seemed longer and steeper than I remembered from any previous encounter. Last year, this area was shrouded in thick fog and there was nothing to be seen, but today, there was no such impediment to view below. The hill dropped away sharply to the sand a long way below, and the curve of Swanage Bay was clearly and beautifully visible. I stopped momentarily to take a quick photo so I could compare it to last year.

There's a problem with the sky not being full of thick fog. It means the sun can shine down completely unattenuated, and it was a hot sun today. The clouds seemed to be getting fewer and farther between, so there were longer stretches of the direct heat on us. It had taken a few miles, but I was just tipping over from comfortably warm to a bit toasty, and I wondered if this heat was the reason I was feeling the effort so much.

Twelve months earlier, the race was on a hot weekend, which wasn't unexpected. After all, if you're going to enter a race in the middle of June, you have to expect it to be at least warm, and possibly "bloody boiling" (to quote Martin from *Friday Night Dinner*). But last year, we'd at least had some suitable conditions to prepare us. The three weeks preceding the race had been rain free, with hot sunshine beating down every day, and I had taken the opportunity to run in the middle of each day to get myself used to the heat. But this year, the weather had been miserable for weeks – months, even – before race weekend, and now we were suddenly hit with uncharacteristically hot weather.

All of this, I hoped, was the reason I was currently feeling so shitty. I never feel great for the first 10 or 15 miles of a long run, but rather than just feeling like I needed to get a bit more "into it", today I felt really sluggish and not right at all. At least I was finally at the top of the hill, which meant I had my first decent descent of the race.

Despite it being downhill, I normally don't find much of a rhythm in this section and to start with, nothing was different today. The path was overgrown, the ground at an annoying slant which made me feel like I was always just a few degrees from twisting my ankle, and I found myself running with my arms up in front of my chest to protect my soft flasks from the spiky bushes encroaching on the path. But then I came to another familiar gate and started down the gravelly hill, which is usually either too muddy (in the winter) or too dusty (in the summer) to run down confidently. But today, it was somehow just *perfect*. I managed to get my cadence and stride in tune with the step sections and, for the first time in the race, I felt like the running was effortless. It gave me time to look around (when I wasn't concentrating on steps), and I was surprised at how many new little diversions there were since last time I'd passed. They were mostly just a few tens of feet, signalled with flapping tape doing a poor job of protecting passers-by from the gaping voids beyond, but it was a stark indication of the changes happening.

The first 6 months of 2024 has been a time of crumbling coasts, most notably around Houns Tout, West Bay and

Charmouth. But it seems the eastern end of the Jurassic Coast wasn't immune either. While sad to see, it's also a natural progression. After all, a mere 10,000 years ago, there was no Lulworth Cove, and Foreland Point, off which proudly stand the stacks of Old Harry Rocks, was joined to the Needles on the Isle of Wight. Erosion made what we have today, and it isn't going to stop just because we've put a pretty little path along the edge.

After a couple of wooded sections where half of the steps were actually tree roots, and a final diversion around another collapsed section of the coastline, at 9:18 am I was running across the grass at the very edge of Swanage town. I went through the collection of holiday homes where I used to get lost, but this year I'd spent some time looking at the map before the race and not only knew the turns to take but had also spotted an alleyway I always missed. Cutting down there not only took me the way the official race GPX showed, but it was also a little shorter than the route I normally ended up taking.

I ran the road section down to the seafront, a little stretch of easy terrain and lovely gently downhill gradients where I usually speed up with ease.

Not today, though.

I was running, but it felt like I had treacle on my shoes. My legs were heavy to lift, and every step was just a bit more effort than I expected. I started to wonder if I was just being silly. Had I set my expectations too high? Was I pushing too hard to get that sub-30 finish? My training hadn't been great, and I wasn't heat acclimated. Maybe I should just ease back a little, stop worrying about the effort and just enjoy myself for an hour or so and see where I stood after that. Yes, that sounded like a much better idea, and one I secretly hoped would give enough time for my body and mind to wake up and let me get back to chasing that target.

It was a sunny and warm Saturday in Summer, which meant that Swanage seafront was busy. Just as I was about to cross the road to avoid the narrow pavement squashed between parked cars and railings above the sea wall, I spotted a guy in running gear, stopped a little way ahead and fiddling with his soft flask. I continued on to investigate, and as I got closer, I realised it was the extra water stop that Justin had mentioned at the briefing, and despite not having drunk much I set about filling up my partly drained soft flask from the big water tank.

The guy who was there when I arrived was having a bit of trouble getting to a tiny plastic funnel that was clipped to his pack, so I helped him out. He used the funnel to fill up his soft flask with what looked like Tailwind powder, and I was intrigued as I'd had a similar idea before the race. I was going to 3D print a funnel for that very reason, but as I watched on at the mess created as the powder seemed to ignore the easy route into the flask and end up all over his hands and blowing around in the air instead, I thought that maybe just pouring from the Tailwind sachets I had would be the better of two evils.

I got going again while the other chap was still fighting with his funnel and passed Justin running towards me with a big, happy smile plastered over his face which I think had been the case every single time I've ever seen him!

"Did you get some water?", he shouted over, suddenly looking a bit concerned that maybe I'd missed his impromptu hydration station in this hot weather.

"Yep, all good. Thanks for sorting that," I replied as we passed each other, and he continued on happy again.

The Banjo Pier passed by on my left, then I made my way along the pedestrianised section of Swanage and headed under the Mowlem Theatre towards Fish & Chip Square. Continuing round onto the old railway tracks embedded in the stone floor, I passed the toilets and considered a stop, but just didn't need them at that moment. It occurred to me that I probably wasn't drinking enough, what with hardly needing a top up 6 miles into the race back along the seafront, and I made the decision to finish one of my soft flasks before Durlston Castle as I knew there were water taps in that area. That was in just a few miles, so I set about glugging from my flask, being careful not to drink too much in one go as I didn't want a stitch, but aiming to make sure that at least one flask was empty in the next 20 minutes or so.

I passed a bunch of the Saturday Morning Kayak Crew, but this year their long boats were on the pavement instead of forming a *Total* Wipeout style obstacle course in front of me as had been the way last time I did this race. Past the pier entrance, I confidently carried on up the short but steep hill towards the single concrete bollard, now knowing the route. A little stretch of flat road, then round the corner to begin the climb up The Downs.

The grass hill is steep enough to make you work, but not so long as to be a huge challenge. As I started up, my walking pace was strong, and I was happy that my hill training had paid off.

21

I was finding it a moderate effort, but not too much, and a couple of glances back showed the people coming up after me getting a further behind each time. With over an hour having passed since I started, I took the opportunity to have half of the Apple Strudel flapjack that I had tucked in my vest. Having never had one before (good practice for race day, right?), I found it quite tasty, but I wouldn't have described it as Apple Strudel. It was more just generic "sweet" flavour with a hint of cinnamon.

With the hill over and now back on tarmac pavement, I picked up pace to a run. It wasn't a very convincing run, my legs still not working as well as they should be, but I kept it going all the way down to the entrance of Durlston Country Park. I'd missed checking the timing point on my chart at the Swanage *Refill* tap as I hadn't bothered to stop, having just filled up with water from Justin's new water stop. I checked my card for the timing at this next spot, the entrance to Durlston. My target was 9:40am, and my watch was telling me I was 1 minute behind, but still 3 minutes ahead of last year. I would have been buoyed, had it not been for the fact that my effort level felt totally unsustainable for another 10 miles, let alone 95.

4

Saturday 22nd June 2024, 09:41

The first part of the Durlston estate is under tree cover, and it was a welcome change from the sunshine beating down from the now almost cloudless sky. I wound my way along the familiar paths and on to Isle of Wight Road which was, in all but name, just a continuation of the gravel tracks in the rest of the estate. It did start to climb though, which ended the running I had been stubbornly continuing and I carried on at a brisk walking pace. Although slightly ahead of last year's times, I was later today in real terms as the race start was a little over 10 minutes after it had been the previous year. This meant that rather than being in the middle of the Durlston Parkrun (like during the Oner in 2022) or catching the tail end like last year, I got a few claps of encouragement from volunteers clearing things up after the event had finished.

There was a bit of a buzz outside Durlston Castle, with parkrun runners and volunteers chatting away as I deliberately detoured from the race route, taking the right-hand side of the castle building and down a steep tarmac path towards the cliffs and water beyond. I stopped part way down outside a wooden shed which had 4 taps that fed into a big trough sink. After waiting for a lady fill up a bowl for the dog, I refilled the soft flask that I had successfully managed to drain in those 20 minutes since starting up the Downs.

I'd known my little detour to the tap would add a stretch of steep downhill, and I could have cheekily continued on down to meet up with the race route, but that would have cut out a few hundred metres, and I don't like knowingly taking the wrong route. It was only a short climb back up to the right route, but I had been dreading it as it really was quite steep. It's funny how your brain can build things up, because when it came to actually *doing* it, my legs felt strong and I again thought that maybe – just maybe – my body and mind were waking up to the idea of this race.

I passed around the outside of the building to the consternation of a couple of people who had watched me go down and then come back up the hill and headed off down another steep track, meeting a few of the very last parkrunners coming up. There was no shade now and the sun was bright and hot, but despite the heat, I finally felt like I had energy! I ran along the gravel path, past the steps up to the Great Globe, and just before I crossed the bottom of the hill back up to those water taps, 4 runners came down from that direction onto the track in front of me.

Far from being annoyed at being "overtaken" by people going the wrong way, it boosted me. I'd added a hill, stopped for water and gone the longer (and correct) route, and yet this group had only just caught up with me. I was definitely picking up pace, which made a grin involuntarily appear on my face. Those first 10-or-so miles were hard work, but now I'd switched into "race mode" and I could get on with enjoying myself!

I tagged on to the back of the group of 4 towards Anvil Point lighthouse. There was Melissa Montague, Sam Dixon, James Tempest and Craig Foley, and as a group, they were running a little slower than I would have liked, but almost certainly at a more sensible and sustainable pace than if I'd been here on my own.

Melissa took the lead at the steep, uneven steps down to the little valley before the lighthouse, and I was getting a bit frustrated at the slow pace. I knew this bit of coast well and although it was a bit sketchy, I usually ran down quickly, skipping across the uneven bits and – so far at least – making it to the bottom in one piece. But today, I was behind a group that were tentatively picking their way to the bottom. Not a bother, I told myself. I needed to keep slow.

At the bottom of the valley, we all started up the rocky path on the other side. Despite putting in the effort, I started lagging behind. There was nothing conscious about it – I wanted to be pushing on, to be running where I could and fast moving everywhere else. But in the space of 2 minutes, my legs had decided they wanted to go back to sleep, and I was struggling to even walk at a decent pace up this not particularly steep climb. As I crested the summit next to the lighthouse, the group of 4 were halfway across the next stretch of grass, a good way ahead of me. And to cement my deluded view of how I might have been picking up the pace, a check of the Anvil Point Lighthouse row on my timing chart showed I'd lost 4 minutes just since the entrance of Durlston. I was now a minute behind my position last year, and I'd actually been feeling like I was doing well through a chunk of that. Something was definitely wrong today.

As I slowly ran along the flat grassy section with my legs feeling worrying like I'd already run 100 miles to get to this point, I picked two electrolyte pills from my vest, stuck them in my mouth and chewed. An eruption of saltiness had me swigging from my flask, but my logic was that if I broke the capsules, the electrolytes would get in my system faster, and I needed *something* to change how I felt. When the salty water was gone, I finished the remainder of the Apple Strudel flapjack. With all this "admin" done, I tuned back into my surroundings to see that I was on my own again, the gang-of-four having disappeared out of sight ahead.

My next timing spot was Dancing Ledge, or rather the fence above the famous coastal spot next to which the South West Coast Path passes, but I was beginning to dread checking my progress. This should really have been a sign to me that it was time to dump the unrealistic (at least today) expectations and just enjoy myself. But instead, I was hung up on the fact that despite it being relatively flat, I seemed to be putting in a lot of effort and hardly moving at all, which was only going to make my times worse.

The overgrown nature of the path in summer means it's never just an easy run, constantly having to try and see through the thick grasses that hide your feet for cracks, ruts and stones that might trip you. I continued on in the sunshine passing a Nautical Mile Marker rising high above me from its massive concrete base and wound my way up and down some small hills, missing the chatter I had last year with Iain at this point when everything felt so easy in comparison. At least, that's how I remembered it.

I passed a stone marker inscribed with "Dancing Ledge" much sooner than I expected, and for a moment, my spirits lifted. Over the next few minutes, I had a reality check as it dawned on me that at the bottom of the stone marker, hidden by vegetation, would have been a distance. A mile? Two miles? I didn't know, but I was still a fair way from that fence above the ledge that marked my timing spot.

After a steep descent and ascent where I had to clamber up a steep grass bank to avoid a family that managed to hog the whole path, I did eventually arrive above Dancing Ledge at 10:25 am. I was now 8 minutes behind my target, and 3 minutes short of last year.

I'd made a huge mistake with my timing chart. My optimistic plan meant that if I wasn't having the very best day – and I really, *really* wasn't today – then I would be behind my target. And when I'm behind, I struggle mentally, the motivation to push on abandoning me when I need it most. Sub-30 was a hopeful "A" target, but my 2023 time had felt pretty much guaranteed, at least in my mind before about 9 o'clock this morning. Now, I was looking at my times for a 6pm finish – just under 34 hours – and beginning to wonder if even that was realistic with how I felt today.

Down in the dumps, I continued on, chastising myself for not just enjoying the day. The *adventure* was what I liked, right? Who gives a shit about times? As much as I tried, I couldn't convince the negative part of my brain, which seemed to take pleasure in reminding me just how tired my legs felt right now on this relatively flat and easy section.

"Alright Rich," came a cheerful voice from behind me, and I turned to see Matt Dalton having caught me up. Definitely not a bad sign, as I'd intended to stay behind Matt for the whole race, and it was nice to have some company. We chatted a bit as we turned inland at Seacombe, but I had to say goodbye as he motored on up the steps while I struggled to lift my feet. These steps always seemed to be harder than I expect, but today, for the first time ever, I actually stopped part way up, holding on to the hand rail and taking a moment to rest.

A mile further on at Winspit, I let a couple of runners pass me before the descent down the steep and uneven steps as I didn't want to hold them up. At the bottom, another runner caught me and almost went the wrong way until I directed him inland which was, counterintuitively, the correct route for the coast path. Another set of steps, and this time I not only stopped part way up but plonked myself down on a step. My breathing was ridiculously heavy, and I felt dizzy. Whilst admiring the beautiful view over Winspit and back along the coast, I decided at this point that my race was over.

Whatever was wrong with me wasn't going away. Even minor uphill sections were battering the life out of me. My breathing was far heavier than it should have been, and my legs felt like lead. Flat and downhill sections were just about OK, but at no point was there any real *flow*, that occasional but wonderful effortless feeling you get when you're just enjoying the progress while something else seems to be doing all the work.

I stood and walked at a snail's pace up the rest of the steps while getting my phone out from my pack. A minute later, I was talking with Eva about picking me up at Kimmeridge. That would be in a few hours, so I didn't commit, but just wanted to chat, hear her voice and check she was OK with the possibility of picking me up and then driving on to Weymouth to get my drop bag and give the tracker back. Deep inside my brain, there was still a little part that held out hope that I'd get over this and find whatever was needed to get going again.

The mile to St Aldhelm's Head is full of overgrown paths and energy-sapping hills, and when I came to the top of the last one and passed the Radar Memorial, I was absolutely ruined. I reminded myself that it was a beautiful area and I should at least *try* to appreciate it, so I turned and looked back for a moment. The beauty was all there – the cliffs, the blue sky, the deep azure sea – but it wasn't lighting a fire in my heart today like it usually did. All I seemed to register was just how much hard work it looked in both directions.

The steps at Emmet's Hill are the stuff of nightmares, but now I'd decided to drop out of the race, I had no goal, there was nothing to fear. Just take one step at a time and I'll have them ticked off in no time. Alright, it would take *some* time… probably quite a lot of time, but I could keep it slow and low effort and it needn't be hard work.

Except it was. The descent was absolutely horrible. My legs were actually shaking and stepping from uneven step to uneven step felt genuinely dangerous. It was a real relief to reach the handrail about halfway down, and I must have shown it on my face as a couple of very fit looking walkers with a dog stormed past going uphill, telling me it wasn't far to the bottom with an edge of pity in their voices.

"Well Done," was the last thing they said as we pass, and it stung a bit. Well done for what? I wasn't going to finish, I'd failed. What I'd done wasn't worth any form of congratulations. I was pissed off, but despite reviewing my decision, I felt like it was out of my hands. My body wasn't playing ball today.

The climb up was surprisingly uneventful. I just climbed each step, pushing the hugely overgrown vegetation out the way as I went. I didn't get out of breath, and my legs didn't get any worse, in fact they felt a lot better going up than during the descent. But when I reached the top, I just didn't have any energy left to run, so I walked on through the tall grass, taking cautious steps again so as not to trip on some unseen obstacle.

After a minute or so of walking, I told myself that I really should be running on this flat path, so slipped into a slow run reminiscent of the sort of staggering, unstable shuffle I can just about manage at the end of 100-mile races. Each time I met a group of people – and there were quite a few – I was the one stepping to the side to let them pass. Usually, it was the other way round, but I was making the most of the little stops along the way as running felt bloody miserable.

The single stile in this section came and went, along with the Royal Marine Memorial Garden, and I soon found myself alongside the gate that would have taken me to Renscombe car park where the first checkpoint was located last year. Due to a serious cliff fall at Houns Tout – which was visible just across the bay of Chapmans Pool below – the coast path had been diverted inland, so this year, the first checkpoint was at a car park just outside the village of Kingston. This diversion added about 2 miles to the coast path distance, but not having to do the out-and-back to the Renscombe car park checkpoint brought the total addition to the actual race down to not much more than a mile.

I checked my watch as I passed the gate – 11:40 am. Now I was 25 minutes behind my target, and 18 minutes behind last year. It didn't matter, though – in fact it helped to justify my decision to quit at Kimmeridge, so I'd just enjoy the journey as much as I could.

The route turned to the right through a gap in the stone wall and down a hill, initially grass but turning to a rocky track as it headed towards a little hamlet where the detour from the original coast path route to Houns Tout began.

I'd let the decision to quit settle for the last few miles. It had bubbled a bit and then turned to cement, so it was time to call Eva and order my evacuation. I unlocked my phone and dialled, but despite being connected for 15 seconds, neither of us could hear anything. A check of the signal strength showed bugger all, so I put my phone away for a minute.

Half of the way through the small group of houses was a left turn, a route I had taken so many times in the past. Today, however, that route would take me to a cliff edge and no further, so the new route was to continue straight ahead, past the remainder of the houses. A few had running water features in their gardens, and the sound of babbling water wasn't helping with the thirst I was feeling, having been metering out my water so as not to run out. I'd almost finished both my water bottles and was considering just how clean the water trickling through a pipe in the wall of one of the houses was. Having decided not to risk it, I took a big swig from one bottle, emptying it in the process – it can't be far, and it was surely better to arrive at the checkpoint empty than to unnecessarily carry water.

I went over a wobbly stile at the end of the road and onto a tree covered rocky path, slippery with water that was trickling down the central channel. Walking up was awkward initially, the low hanging branches meaning I was stooped while trying to find footing on the wet rocks, but this didn't last long and I was soon walking uphill on a smooth grassy path.

A second attempt at calling Eva was successful, and I organised my exfiltration plan from Kimmeridge. My stupid little timing chart said I was supposed to be there before 1 pm, so I said I'd aim for 2 pm and told her I'd make my way up to the toll booth so she didn't have to pay the £6 for a 2-minute stop in the car park to pick me up.

While chatting on the phone, I had inadvertently followed a nice stone wall, and it was only when I hung up and looked at my watch that I realised I'd gone the wrong way. I about turned and, in the distance, saw a walker with a big backpack going the correct way – a pretty much dead-straight line in the way I had been going originally, so why I turned at the wall, I have no idea!

I almost caught up with the walker before a gate, which was a little boost for me in showing that, although I wasn't running, my walking pace wasn't too slouchy. When I got to the gate, I passed a group of people who spotted my race number.

"Oh my gosh!" said the lady, in the poshest accent I've ever heard by someone not taking the piss. "One hundred miles, all the way to Exmouth?"

"That's right, although I'm only going as far as Kimmeridge," I started. I just couldn't enjoy the amazement

32

of "normal" people today, not when I was quitting soon. It felt disingenuous to act like I was going to be doing the whole of this epic journey today.

The route from here to the checkpoint was easy now, almost entirely one road a little uphill to the village of Kingston. When I reached the village, I passed a house with a For Sale sign hanging outside and wondered what sort of price these beautiful little cottages would fetch. It turns out to be quite a lot – that small 3-bedroom, 2-bathroom terraced property was on the market for £625,000!

A few minutes later, and after checking my watch a couple of times to make sure I was still on track and wasn't wandering down someone's driveway, I found the entrance to the Houns Tout car park. Straight ahead was a van set up with a table full of goodies, ready for the arrival of the Jurassic Coast ultrarunners.

5

Some sort of miracle

Saturday 22nd June 2024, 12:18

ndy Imms was waiting at the table as I pulled up with my two floppy soft flasks in hand and got chatting.

I'd spoken with Andy back at the start, where I found out he'd won the 120-mile race in 2022 with a Fastest Known Time along the South Haven Point to Exmouth stretch of the coast path. That accolade was snatched from him by Daryl Smith last year, but he planned to do the 120 again this year and, with help from Daryl, get back the FKT on the route. It was not to be, however. With the removal of the 120-mile option, Andy decided not to do the race, instead opting to help out, and so after a stretch of tail-running he was now manning the checkpoint in Houns Tout car park.

I filled my bottles and distributed a whole sachet of Tailwind between them. If low energy was part of the reason for why I was feeling so tired, I might as well pull everything out the bag now. I ate a packet of salt and vinegar crisps, some orange segments and a few bits of melon while also trying to reseat the full water bottles in my race vest and chatting to Andy about my decision to end the race at Kimmeridge. He did a good job of trying to convince me to keep going, and there was a big part of me that prayed that things would turn around.

But I'd never been this far into a race – over 18 miles – and still felt so bad, so I wasn't holding out much hope.

"Let's hope for some sort of miracle, then I can carry on!" I shouted back, as I made my way away from the checkpoint along the path towards Houns Tout about 10 minutes after arriving.

I was now 44 minutes behind my target time, but who's counting? Me. I was still counting. Like an idiot.

This was new territory for me. I'd never been on this bit of path before, but even with my tragic sense of direction, I couldn't possibly go wrong. It was almost a straight line back to the coast, and the route that had taken me to the checkpoint had also taken me up pretty much all of the elevation, so this final stretch was essentially flat. I didn't feel like running to start with, but when the path opened out with expansive views over to Chapmans Pool and Swyre Head – the highest point on the Isle of Purbeck – I couldn't help but feel a bit more energetic and took up a slow jog along the grass.

I reached the top of Houns Tout 20 minutes after leaving the checkpoint, which, interestingly, still had me 44 minutes behind my target time. So, for the last 20 minutes, I'd been at my optimistic race pace, which was a surprise to me. No cause for celebration, but it did give me a little spark of hope that I might still get a reprieve from feeling rubbish.

There was a T junction at the end of the path. The old coast path route that climbed those steps up the hill was to the left – the steps that was no longer there. Whoever manages this stretch of coast path made it really, *really* clear that you didn't want to go left with great wooden boards across the top, some way towards getting covered with vegetation, along with warning signs not to even think about trying to make it down the hill. Not a problem for me – I was turning right anyway.

I got a bit confused for a moment, going a long way round a stone bench at the top of the hill down towards Kimmeridge before I recognised the route, and then started the steep descent west. I ran down, primarily because as uncomfortable as running was, it was more pleasant than walking when the downhill gradient was this steep.

As the slope levelled off to a slightly more comfortable gradient, I lifted my head from concentrating on the immediate path ahead and spotted a massive, dispersed group of people coming towards me on the narrow path. At first I thought they might be Duke of Edinburgh kids, but as I got closer I could see it was a group of older walkers, all very cheerful and making good progress towards the climb I'd just come down. When the first chap spotted me, he called back and the little groups started squeezing into the sides to let me pass, which meant only one thing: I had to keep running, whether I liked it or not!

"You've got gaiters, you're a professional!" shouted one guy as I passed.

"They're brilliant! Keep all the little annoying stones out," I yelled back in reply. I love my gaiters.

I got encouragement from a few more people, and one guy even clapped as I went past, which had me smiling and laughing in thanks. It wasn't long before I was the other side of the whole group, so I could finally stop running.

But... I didn't. At least not immediately.

Running was feeling reasonably tolerable, quite different to the horrible experience of an hour or so ago, so I just kept going until the path became so overgrown it was downright dangerous to run as I would have almost certainly ended up tripping on something hidden in the undergrowth.

The camber of the path became awkward again, then the overgrown vegetation reached another level as I descended a set of steps into what I remember being like a little glade area. My memory had a picture of a few trees, some damp ground, green leaves growing up either side of the path, but today the leaves really were *everywhere*! I was having to push through tall plants, trusting that the path was somewhere ahead of me as I couldn't see the ground at all. I came to another small collapsed section of the path where it wasn't immediately obvious how to get around it, so I took the only option which was to climb up a short but steep hill and then spotted hints of a path into more dense vegetation.

Eventually, I came to the set of steps which took me back up to the normal path, but halfway up I heard some voices ahead. I couldn't *see* the people yet as everything was still so overgrown, and as I went, I was wondering if I would be able to squeeze into the side or whether I'd have to go back the way I came to find a passing spot. When I finally got to the source of the voices, I found a couple who didn't look best pleased with how the path quality was degrading.

"Is there much of this?" the lady asked, a bit annoyed.

"It's quite overgrown for the next couple of hundred metres," I explained, "then it gets back to normal." This seemed to cheer them up a bit, and we did manage to squeeze past each other to get on with our respective journeys. Less than a minute later, I was back on a much less overgrown path, hard baked mud with huge cracks forming the floor, and regular bushes to the sides, far easier to move along than the last few hundred metres.

I had a bit under 3 miles to go to Kimmeridge, and despite being able to run on that downhill section a few minutes before, I seemed to be unable to get going again now. The path undulated, and on one longer section of gentle climb, I found myself sitting down on the ground, not really having made a conscious decision to do so. I sat there for a minute or so, looking back the way I'd come, enjoying the view and beginning to wonder just *why* I had decided to stop. I felt fine, not puffed out, and my legs even felt vaguely awake. The sight of an approaching runner got me back on my feet, and I joined up with Alex Loach, chatting away as we did a combination of running and walking on our way to Kimmeridge.

It was nice to have some company, and I found myself running far more than I would have if I was on my own. I'd explained my decision to quit at Kimmeridge, and Alex wasn't taking it all that seriously, suggesting that maybe I should just carry on.

And I started to wonder why that wasn't the best idea.

I spent a moment thinking about what was coming. Yes, there were the Lulworth Ranges, a particularly tough section, but I had all day to do it if I was no longer chasing any target. And if it turned out to be the wrong decision to continue, I could definitely make it to Weymouth – even if it took the rest of the day – where I could get a burger and a couple of pints, then get the train home. That would make a DNF much less logistically challenging. And, did I mention, I'd get a burger and couple of pints?

And my legs felt… dare I say… good?

"I think you're right. I think I'm going to carry on," I said to Alex after my contemplations.

"Yeahhh! I knew you would!" he replied cheerfully, like I'd finally seen sense, and I couldn't very well change my mind now I'd said it out loud.

"I'm just going to test my legs out, see how they feel," I explained as we descended the path down towards a little wooden bridge. I picked up the pace, but not to the sort of shuffling run that I had been doing over the last few hours. Instead, I found myself doing a proper *run*. I crossed the bridge, and started leaping up the other side, bounding over the uneven section of the hill until I was about two-thirds of the way to the top. I was puffed out, but my legs had worked! I turned back and yelled "Yippeee!" towards Alex, who was far too busy making his way along the path to notice my stupid shouting.

I was back, baby! Screw Kimmeridge, I was going to get this *done*!

There was now the small matter of calling off my rescue party, so I pulled out my phone and dialled Eva. The call didn't connect. I retried, and got the same result, so I sent a message:

If you haven't left, stay at home for now xx

It made sense to me, but at the time, it didn't occur to me that it wasn't a particularly clear message. I called my daughter and managed to get connected, but she was out of the house and didn't know whether Eva had left or not, so I left instructions to let her know I was carrying on with the race. I wouldn't be able to relax until I knew that Eva wasn't waiting for me at Kimmeridge but was instead on her way back home.

I kept trying, and at just after 1:30 pm I got a brief connection, but the call quality was so poor I wasn't sure I'd managed to get the message through. I gave up for now and hoped I could get a decent connection at Kimmeridge.

A familiar red brick pill box passed by 5 minutes later, and a little later Clavell Tower came into view, being far more visible than it had been last year in the fog. I knew I was only a few minutes from Kimmeridge, and I picked up pace and carried on running along the clifftop.

Clavell Tower passed by at 1:42 pm, putting me 52 minutes behind target, but that didn't matter. I was feeling *good* now, and if I could keep up a similar pace to last year, I reckoned eventually I could catch up with my previous time. Things were looking up, and I was feeling so much better, some comfortable running popping up occasionally and a smile and even a laugh or two as I ran along.

I descended the steep steps onto the slipway road at Kimmeridge and started a determined walk up to the toilet block at the top, with its outside tap for refilling my water bottle. On a mission now, I pulled a stick of Tailwind from the back of my pack, opened one of my empty bottles and carefully poured half the contents in, then repeating with the other side. By the time I got to the toilet block, I had two bottles in hand, ready for water.

Once I'd filled the bottles and got them back in my vest, I got my phone out to try contacting Eva again. There were two missed calls, and a message:

What do you want me to do?

I tried calling again with no success, so sent a message back:

Feeling a little better. Will carry on to Weymouth. If I stop there I will get the train back. Hopefully carry on.

Fingers crossed that would sort everything out and I could stop worrying. I'd check the Life360 tracking app we used soon and hopefully see her driving back home.

I made use of the conveniences, then headed off towards the car park, with Alex having overtaken me again after all my faffing. I headed through the car park, not stopping at the food trailers this year as I wasn't going to pay £3.50 for a 500ml bottle of Sprite again! Soon, I'd passed the entrance to the beach, past the house with the perpetually filled washing line and was on my way up towards the UKs longest running oil well. A quick check of my phone showed a message from Eva saying "Ok", and I could see her heading back home on my phone map, so now I could finally relax and enjoy the race.

6

Saturday 22nd June 2024, 13:56

Had I made a mistake? I didn't feel *quite* as enthusiastic as I had 20 minutes before, and as I approached the gate to the Lulworth Ranges, the size of the hills I was soon to climb played on my mind. Over the next 10 miles, there were 7 huge lumps to get over, and then a further 10 miles to Nothe Fort, which suddenly started to seem like a massive ask from my legs which were beginning to protest a little again.

Still, the wonderful thing about situations like this is that I now had absolutely no choice whatsoever. I'd blown my chance at a pickup, so my earliest end point was Weymouth, and there was nothing I could do about it... which, from decision standpoint, made it delightfully simple! No matter how much things ached or how slowly I went, I was getting to Weymouth. And the thought of nipping to the pub after I'd finished was a definite plus point.

Onwards then: next stop, Lulworth, in – according to my watch – 6.4 miles. So, at 1:56 pm on this sunny Saturday afternoon, I crossed through the swing gate under rolls of razor wire and onto the Lulworth Ranges.

Alex and I had ended up together again and we talked away as we made our way along the flat gravel track and across a couple of cattle grids, sticking between the yellow marker posts so as not to accidentally tread on some unexploded ordnance and end up with a *real* excuse not to finish the race. I stopped to faff around with something in my pack and get my poles out for the upcoming climbs while Alex continued on, and by the time I'd made my way slowly up a fairly minor grassy hill, he was quite a long way ahead and getting close to the start of the proper hills. My legs were now complaining on even the slightest hill again, and by the time I made it to the zigzag point halfway up the first (and gentlest) of the seven climbs, Alex was nowhere to be seen.

Being a notable point on the route map, this zigzag was another of my timing points, and here I learnt I was now almost an hour behind my target. It was now officially time to stop worrying about the 30-hour target, and instead I decided to focus on my 2023 time. I was still a long way behind – 42 minutes right now – but at least that one wouldn't run away from me *quite* as fast, and if my mind and body decided to actually cooperate at any point today, I could try and chase it down.

The few minutes of steep climb wiped away any enthusiasm I might have had, and instead I started trying to decide which type of burger and pint I would get in Weymouth before getting the train back home. The hill was horrible – although fairly short, it was brutally steep, and my legs screamed at me. Even my breathing started becoming a bit ragged again, and at one point I wondered if I'd actually make it to the top or keel over in a heap beforehand.

Of course I did make it, helped in part by knowing that the next mile or so afterwards was a much gentler climb. After a gate, the first section traced a line around the top of a steep valley down to the cliffs above Brandy Bay, then gradually climbed above Gad Cliff before dropping steeply down to the bottom of Worbarrow Tout, a promontory on the eastern end of Worbarrow Bay. It took me 20 minutes of mostly walking to cover the one-and-a-quarter miles of this easier stretch, with a few running attempts peppered in that didn't really amount to anything. I felt I was very much back to putting in the effort but getting no real effect, just plodding along still fervently trying to figure out the puzzle of just why nothing seemed to be working as it should today.

Having circumnavigated a small stretch around the back of the beach at Worbarrow Bay, I was on a flat section of grass that started increasing in gradient until it formed the climb up to Flower's Barrow. I've yet to be convinced that any climb on the South West Coast Path is as steep for so long. There are plenty taller but with gentle gradients, and a few steeper but very short, but this hill has a combination that makes you desperate to reach the end, only to crane your head back to look upwards and see you aren't even halfway up yet!

From my vantage point at the bottom, I could see a train of 4 people climbing up, evenly spaced, seeming to be hardly moving.

And then I started up the steep bit.

I passed a couple with a dog. This was the early stage; I had a little bit of strength at this point.

About a third of the way up, I sat down and enjoyed the view back. My legs were screaming, and my brain was telling me to just have a rest – as long as I wanted, time didn't matter. The couple with the dog had just caught up to me when I decided to continue up.

I stopped about two thirds of the way up, and repeated the procedure, again waiting for the dog to snuffle its way up to my position.

Almost at the top, I stopped again, feeling a bit dizzy. As I kept meeting the dog-people, I had a little chat with them as they approached. We both agreed that this was an absolute beast of a hill.

I passed through the gate at the top, now 48 minutes behind my 2023 time – 6 minutes lost since the zigzag just a couple of miles before. I wished I could stop thinking about the bloody time – it wasn't useful in the slightest, and yet here I was, clinging on to numbers which did nothing but depress me.

There's a stretch of about a quarter of a mile of flat ground past the Iron Age fort at Flower's Barrow, so I tried my best to muster up the energy to run, but no speed materialised. There was no motivation, no energy. I felt again like I was plodding through the last few miles of a 100-mile race, and yet here I was, only twenty-something miles in.

Arish Mell is a little bay sandwiched between two steep 500-foot climbs. It's a beautiful bay with huge rising chalk cliffs to the sides, only slightly marred by the now disused Winfrith nuclear power station waste pipe that runs out to sea. The beauty, however, didn't cheer me up much as I descended down towards the sea, because as had been the case over the last few hours on steep descents, it was a bloody miserable experience. I was running because it would get it over and done with quicker than walking, which would be equally as horrible but just take longer. My poles were doing as much of the work as possible, stabbing the ground in front of me so my arms could take some of the pressure of the descent instead of it all being distributed between my toes and my quads. Halfway down, a short flat section was a huge relief to my legs and now also my arms which had decided to now join the screaming party.

I got to the bottom, but the last section of steeper, gravelly tracks didn't feel particularly safe. I didn't have the energy or strength to sort out any missteps or slips on the loose stones, but thankfully my feet somehow found a safe route down.

I usually use the momentum of the descent to carry me about the first 10 metres up the other side before I run out of steam, but today I didn't even bother running and just walked across the concrete section that provided a path across the nuclear waste pipe and began the slog up the western side.

My glacial pace and a couple of stops to "admire the view" saw me being caught by Jay King, who was making his way steadily up the hill behind me. We chatted a bit, and then seemed to drop into a similar pace up the remainder of the hill, which thankfully started to level out. I passed another of my timing points, and despite having maintained a pace that felt like I was hardly moving, I found I was now 45 minutes behind my 2023 time. Somehow, I'd managed to gain 3 minutes since Worbarrow Bay. The emotional rollercoaster had just started a small but definite climb.

The hill up from Arish Mell is steep to start with then drops down to a much more sensible gradient – where we now were – but that latter section goes on and on for what seems like forever. In reality, it's only about a mile, but after having the energy kicked out of you by the Flower's Barrow hill, then the Arish Mel hill, there's usually not much left to get up any sort of pace for the slightly uphill final stretches to the highest point east of Lulworth. Jay and I eventually made it to the top, marked with a little brick building covered in antennae, and we started to mix between running and walking down the white chalky track that took us towards the end of the Ranges.

We were getting close to the checkpoint at Lulworth now, and I was getting a psychological boost at the prospect of some coffee – the first caffeine I would have had for 2 weeks. I would normally wait until later in the evening, and my original plan had been to have coffee at Nothe Fort, but I needed all the help I could get now so had decided to pop in the performance enhancing drug a little earlier.

Once we passed through the gate signalling the end of the Lulworth Ranges, I broke into a run. It was an incredibly slow, shuffling run, no style, no substance, and no real speed... but it *was* a run. The soft grass was at the perfect downhill gradient that meant there was absolutely no justification for walking, the running here was going to be about as effortless as running could be.

It wasn't effort-less, but it wasn't *too* bad. I had the buzz that came with the closeness to a checkpoint – a stop, a rejuvenation, some food, coffee, and a couple of paracetamol tablets to dull the pain in my back where my pack had already started rubbing the skin raw. It's a regular problem for me, and

I really should stop writing the same thing about it and get myself another bloody pack[2]!

I turned to the right in line with the trace on my watch and started the final steep descent towards the checkpoint. It wasn't as long as the previous downhills, and I wanted to get to that village hall as quickly as possible, so I sucked up the misery, put my faith and weight against my poles and styled-out something akin to falling down a steep hill towards one of the two wooden gates I knew led down to the final metal gate below which took me out onto the road.

A few minutes later, at 3:54 pm, I stepped through the door of Checkpoint 2 at the West Lulworth Village Hall.

---

[2] I have news! I have bought another pack. It's a Inov8 Racepac 20 – as recommended by Matt Dalton – and it looks bloody lovely. Loads of useful pockets, lots of space, padding in places that matter. Fingers crossed it lives up to how it looks.

7

Saturday 22nd June 2024, 15:54

"Do you want just cheese?" asked the cheerful lady in the kitchen at the village hall.

"Er…," I stammered, my brain a bit mashed with the transition from running to standing still. "What are the options?"

"Cheese. Ham. Cheese and ham. That's about it."

"Cheese and ham sounds lovely, thank you."

That cheerful lady was Lou Gillard, who will pop up a lot more in this story, and somehow always managed to be upbeat and happy. Her joyful demeanour perked up my spirits a bit, and I was smiling as I headed back to the table I'd dumped my bag on, carrying a cheese and ham sandwich and a cup of strong coffee.

I went back up to the table with the squidgy cup from my pack and had 3 cups of squash before returning to devour the sandwich. It was good. White slice, thick cheese, plenty of butter and a nice slice of ham. Exactly what I was after. During ultras, I can eat savoury all day (as long as I've had enough fluids), but sweet stuff tends to start disagreeing within the first couple of hours.

"Can I fill those up for you," came a voice from beside me. My bottles went off after I'd dug a sachet of Tailwind out of my pack with the instructions to just randomly slap it in the bottles. Apparently, people had been getting really picky and a bit rude about exact amounts in bottles during the day, which surprised me. I thought all ultrarunners were a cheerful happy-go-lucky bunch (at least for the first 50 miles), but no, there are some grumpies out there. Don't be a grump – everyone's just trying to help.

I'd finished my sandwich, drunk half the coffee, gone back for more squash and was just digging out a couple of paracetamol pills when my bottles came back ready to stick back in my pack.

Jay had come into the hall and was doing his "admin". I used that term earlier in this book, and I shamelessly nicked it from Jay, because it just nails what you're up to. "Admin", in this instance, was everything from filling water bottles to changing clothes to sorting food to taping feet. All the stuff you have to get done when you're not running.

I didn't care about time anymore, and I wasn't paying attention to my watch, but there came a natural point where I reached the end of everything I wanted to get done and it just felt like time to go. That was pretty much on the 15-minute mark, not too bad for a relaxed stop at a checkpoint, and so at just before ten past four I was making my way out the door and back down the road.

Now, this next section is tough, and I knew it. Almost certainly the toughest 3 miles on the whole race, maybe the whole of the South West Coast Path. But I had a few secret weapons. I'd had coffee, after a long abstinence from caffeine.

That would help. And I'd had paracetamol, which would start working its magic soon, dulling the aches and pains.

But there was one more thing.

On Wednesdays for most of the previous couple of months, I'd finished work and driven over to Church Road in Lulworth, where the Village Hall that hosts the checkpoint happens to be situated and, more importantly, is a spot where it's free to park. I'd get out the car, don my race vest and proceed to run the next 3 miles of the race route, but with a bit of a twist.

It's a hilly route, with 4 decent sized hills, so what better thing to do than double up the hills? What I mean by "double up" is that you run up the first hill, and just as you reach the top, turn around and run back down again. Then walk back up – because, by now, your body has decided you're an idiot, so it won't run any more – and when you reach the top for the second time, just carry on to the next descent, where, when you reach the bottom, turn around and head back up. Yes, it is fucking mad… but it wasn't my idea – blame Pat Robbins for this one! If you discount the flat mile to and from the car to the first hill, you get a whopping 4,000ft of climb in just 8 miles.

All that training was supposed to do 2 things. Firstly, in theory, it would "make my legs and my mind strong", which, judging by the last 30-odd miles, was absolute bollocks. But more importantly right now, it gave me an intricate knowledge of every footfall of the next 3 miles – the remaining hilly bit of the race essentially from here until about West Bay, some 35 miles further on. Get this done, and it was plain sailing!

So off I went down the pavement from the village hall, safe in the knowledge that I didn't have to check my watch for a

51

while, but somewhat less safe because of the knowledge of just what lay ahead. I crossed the road, went through a field, took a left turn after climbing some steps, then trundled along an overgrown path to the bottom of the first hill, all in a sort-of jaunty walk-jog style that began to suggest that I might be back in that "enjoying myself" headspace. Considering what was in store, this was a very strange place to feel like that.

I took the popular (and correct) chalk path up the hill. In training, I'd taken the grassy route to the right-hand side which was both steeper and taller and took me past the tumulus, the highest point on the hill (obviously – it was a training run, right?). So, this chalk path should have been easier than the steeper grass path.

And it was. No drama.

The coffee was kicking in.

The paracetamol was kicking in.

The intricate knowledge of the path was kicking in.

I was in charge!

For the first third, anyway.

Then, as a 400ft climb always was, it turned out to be quite hard work by the top. I took solace in the fact that I even in the heat, even as tired as I felt, I was still overtaking lots of people, trying to ignore the fact that they were here for a day out instead of an ultramarathon. At the top of the hill, it got decidedly annoying with the masses of people that were in the way. Did they not know that I was in a race? I had to detour onto the grass on occasions, deviating from the racing line… which made about as much difference as adding a few metres to 105 miles. Not much then, but it still made me irrationally and unjustifiably cross.

I could feel a gentle energy from the coffee as I reached the gate that led onto the path down towards Durdle Door – a path that could have been a London street at rush hour. Strip away the Great British clouds and turn the heat up to a level where any self-respecting European would probably still have a jumper on, and everyone and their dog (literally) come to places that are publicised (mostly on social media) as being worth visiting. But the end result is a bunch of sweaty adults, feral kids and hot, bored-looking dogs between you and the thing that's worth visiting. Come back in November. Or February. On a dull, grey Thursday. At 10am. Then you get to see what the place is really like, all on your own.

The slope down to Durdle Door is quite steep and a little slippery with loose stones, so although it was busy, about half of the people were being quite tentative going either up or down. There were gaps, I had energy, and it felt like a bit of an opportunity to get past everyone, so with the help of my poles I jogged down, skipping across the cracks in the path and jumping between the jutting rocks. It ended up being quite a fun experience until I reached the bottom, and found it was so busy that even my usual "out of the way" paths far away from the views were blocked with dawdling people!

I got onto the highest path past Durdle Door, running along the top and enjoying the view of the big arch. She was big today – sometimes when I passed by the rocks looked small and distant, far out to sea and almost insignificant. Today, however, was one of those days where the Drinking Dragon[3] looked so close I could have reached out and scraped my

---

[3] Take a look at a photo of Durdle Door and with some imagination, you'll spot a dragon popping its head in the sea to drink some water.

fingers on the rough surface. I've no idea why it looks different each time – almost certainly psychological expectation – but I enjoyed it, always wondering what I was going to experience at this spot I'd passed maybe 50 times before.

Slightly less enjoyable was checking my timing chart and finding out I was now 56 minutes behind my 2023 time. Because I didn't know what time I should have left Lulworth, I had no idea how my speed over the last mile or two post-checkpoint compared with last time, but I was almost an hour behind my *secondary* target which didn't sit particularly well. Still, I reviewed myself and found I felt OK. The coffee was definitely perking me up mentally, nothing was hurting (thanks, paracetamol), and I knew what was coming – lumps and bumps, but ones I'd done so many times before that they almost felt like friends now.

The dip beyond Durdle Door is called Scratchy Bottom (go on, you can snigger!), and the climb after this is quite something. It's not long in the scheme of big hills, but it's steep enough such that by about half of the way up, you're begging for the top. Even with all that practice, it wasn't easy, but I found myself at the summit, and for a moment it felt strange – wrong even – to carry on. I was so used to turning around at this point, running back down and then climbing the hill again that it was a real delight to actually make progress!

I ran down the next hill. It wasn't pleasant, but I ran. And I didn't feel like I was going to fall over, or that I was out of control at all. All in all, it felt pretty good for a steep descent 30-odd miles into a race.

The next climb up to Bat's Head was tolerable – steep like the last, but again, I was appreciating the fact that I didn't have to do it twice. However, this climb became much gentler about halfway to the top, then just dragged on for a while. Jay, who I'd been jostling with for position since Arish Mel, was catching me on the uphill sections, but I was building up a bit of a gap on the downhills, which is a familiar story for me on these hills.

After this next descent, I was at the bottom of the hill to White Nothe – the last really big bugger of a hill from here until West Bay. With caffeine in my system, I had the motivation and enthusiasm to get to the top, but my legs really hated me at this point. And it was whilst climbing this final hill that I decided, despite it being pretty flat all the way to West Bay, my day would be done at Weymouth where I would indulge in a couple of pints of Doom Bar and some greasy grub.

My mind was happy at this point. It had caffeine and was working pretty well. My legs were not, and they wanted nothing more than to stop right now and not move again for several days. Between the two of them, a deal was reached, and I felt very happy that a stop at Weymouth was a decent but sensible effort. Despite something feeling very wrong with my overall performance, I'd tried – even to the point of aborting on a previous attempt to DNF at Kimmeridge. I'd made a valiant effort: 40-odd miles would be a good shout.

Jay and I climbed slowly up the hill, joined by Chris Scott, and we all worked our way up to the obelisk at about the same pace. A guy running down the other way congratulated us, which was nice at it looked like he meant it – I got the sense from his gear, form and smile that he knew the area and had a sense of what we were up against.

I passed the obelisk, and this year, I didn't crawl behind into the shade to lay down for 5 minutes in an attempt to stave off something approaching heat-stroke. Maybe that was because it was 5:12 pm, and I was 45 minutes down on the 2023 time.

Wait, what? *45 minutes?*

At Durdle Door, I was 56 minutes behind. In a few miles of tough terrain, I'd made up 11 minutes. This was promising, and gave me a good boost, especially now that it was flat for a while and I would soon – hopefully – be able to actually enjoy the decent downhill stretch that was coming up.

Jay and I ran along the path past White Nothe and the cottages, and a mile or so later we both commented on how nice the view was from the gate above Burning Cliff which captured the curved stretch of Weymouth and Portland.

At the bottom of the hill, I guided Jay down the not-so-obvious South West Coast Path route ahead, a narrow stretch between two fences that led straight ahead despite the SWCP marker pointing to the right. Both options were the official coast path, it's one of those spots where it splits in two directions, but I was happy as I knew we were not only on the correct race route but it was also shorter and flatter than the alternative route to the right.

Once we got on the longer downhill stretch to Ringstead, I pulled away from Jay, enjoying the rare feeling (at least today) of easy downhill running. The terrain was perfect – tarmac road or fairly flat trail, all with a gentle downhill gradient. And what's more, I knew that at the bottom there was a cafe that sold ice creams and drinks!

I was enjoying the downhill and the first flickers of "maybe…" started sparking up in my brain. A different part countered by shouting about the pint and burger that I'd miss out on if I carried on at Weymouth. I let the two factions inside my brain have a wrangling match while I just concentrated on making progress and not tripping over anything.

The path levelled off as it reached pretty much sea level, then turned to the right and took me past a whole load of holiday caravans, a few cottages and then to a T-junction. To the left, the South West Coast Path and the route of my race. But to the right, Ringstead Cafe. No competition, really.

Last year, I'd followed Darren Curtis-White here to the café and got a can of Diet Coke and a Calippo. I'd been looking forward to it since the obelisk back at White Nothe, when most of the hard work was done for a while.

But when I was within sight of the building, I was dismayed to see all the hatches and doors were closed. There was a man sealing up the last of the shutters, and I asked if they were closed – a bit of a silly question really, but I was hoping it might just *look* closed, but actually be open for another 15 minutes as it was quarter to six now.

"What did you want?" he asked.

"A can of coke and an ice cream," I replied, hopefully.

I followed him round to the far side of the building, where he called inside to the people cleaning up and shutting everything down. Luck was on my side, and a few minutes later I was back outside with my New Forest Ice Cream version of a Calippo and a can of ice-cold Diet Coke.

The can disappeared in 2 gulps – a risky strategy if you're running fast, but not when you're doing a combination of walking and shuffling. It was absolutely delicious, the coldness countering the heat of the day, and the flavour something

57

different from slightly sugary and salty Tailwind drink. I binned the can and ripped the top off the lolly, having had some trouble doing this last year while running along. Four minutes after turning right at that T junction, I was passing the same turn but heading the correct way now. Sam Carden, the race photographer, was waiting on the approach to Ringstead Bay and got a shot of me holding the not-a-Calippo and smiling like I was actually *enjoying* myself.

And to be honest, I was. Enjoying myself, that is. Not only had I had a fun run down to Ringstead, a nice drink and an ice-cold lolly in my hand, but when I reached that T-junction for the second time, I'd checked my time and found I was now *40* minutes behind 2023. I'd made up 16 minutes since Durdle Door on my progress last year, which was a huge motivation! I was ignoring the fact that some of those 16 minutes was gained by me not laying down behind the obelisk like last year, but I was taking solace from every positive I could. And it was having a dangerous effect. I was starting to sway towards the idea of *not* stopping at Weymouth.

The path took me behind the beach at Ringstead and onto a shaded gravel track that would carry me to Osmington Mills. It was mostly flat, the occasional little lump, and once I finished the ice lolly, I picked up pace a little. Rounding a corner, I met up with Jay again.

"Where did you go?" he asked, surprised to see me.

"I stopped back at the cafe, just caught it before it closed but managed to get a coke and ice cream."

"Awww, I wish I'd done that!" said Jay, sounding dismayed. "I really fancy a really cold Coke."

"Well, we go through the pub in about a mile, we could call in?" I suggested.

And so that's what we did, once we'd ticked off the remainder of the path, past the observation post at Bran Point, across a grassy field and through a gate which led into the back of the pub garden.

I've walked and run through the Smuggler's Inn at Osmington Mills a good number of times, but until today, I'd never passed through the doors into the pub itself. It was a quaint place, lots of wood and low ceilings, which shouldn't have surprised me having researched its history a little for previous books. There was also the sense of it being reasonably high-end or, being less charitable, remote enough to charge a fairly high price for bog-standard fayre – I honestly don't know which. There was a sign by the door asking us to wait to be seated, but we ignored that and headed straight to the bar in front of us.

There were quite a few people at the bar, but we were served quickly which I was very thankful for. I'd already stopped for 4 minutes at Ringstead, and conscious of knocking down that gap between my time this year and last year, I wanted to get moving. Jay got his ice-cold Coke from a little bottle, and poured it over ice in a glass, and I got a pint of water with ice.

"That'll be £3.50 please," said the guy behind the bar to Jay. Wow – that beat my Sprite last year at Kimmeridge! They were the same price, but my bottle was 500ml, whereas Jay's pretty little glass Coke bottle was only 330ml. I'm such a tight arse, aren't I!

Outside the pub, we both started up the road heading inland, inventively called Mills Road, which would take us back onto the proper coast path after a few minutes. I was still buzzing. I felt tired, but I was finally *allowed* to feel tired – I'd covered 37 miles and climbed 6,500 feet, so unlike earlier in the day, it was *normal* to feel knackered and for everything to ache a bit. But I also had the optimism that came from that time difference with last year ticking down, giving me a sense that I was going relatively quickly. The day wasn't cool yet, but it was definitely less hot than it had been, and with all the fluids I'd just consumed, I think I was finally starting to sort out any issues with heat – maybe that had been the problem all along?

I checked with Jay that he knew where he was going, then I sped up my walking pace going up the gentle hill, and by the time I'd turned onto the path again, I was back on my own.

I can never remember the details of this section, but there were a set of steps where each wasn't tall, but there were a lot of them, so I was relieved when I was at the top. Then fields – diagonal tracks across grass, tracks around the edge of fields, and a few nondescript ups and downs. There was the big PGL Adventure Centre, which I could tick off as I passed around its perimeter fence and I knew I was getting closer to Weymouth but couldn't for the life of me remember how far it was to the town.

On this stretch between Osmington Mills and Bowleaze on the edge of Weymouth, there have been times where it seems to pass by quickly for me, and other times where it's really dragged. Today was one of the former, and I unexpectedly found myself on the 3 sharp turns that took me around the Riviera Hotel and then through Fantasy Island.

It was 6:43 pm and, despite the stop in the pub with Jay, I was now just 38 minutes behind my time last year, a further 2 minutes in the bank. I was moving really well, and all this confirmation of my progress made me try harder, push more, and aim to get that time down even more.

I made my way over the grassy hill above Furzy Cliff, down past the Harvester pub and onto the start of the long promenade that led into town. I now swapped over to the back of my first credit-card sized laminated timing chart to get the "detailed" numbers for Weymouth.

I am quite obsessive about timing[4], but there was a good reason for the detailed section coming into Weymouth. Just before the checkpoint at Nothe Fort, there is a lifting bridge which opens every 2 hours between 10 am and 6 pm in order to let Boaty McBoatface and friends through. Had I managed to stick to my 2024 target times, I would have arrived just minutes before the 6 pm lift, so I would have needed to know when to push hard to make sure I didn't get held up for 10 minutes while the priority was given to the mariners over the runners.

Obviously, the bridge timing was irrelevant now as I was so late that whoever was in charge of lifting it had driven home, had a bath, had dinner and was settling down with a beer in front of the "1% Club". I quickly did the mental maths to adjust the times for where I was now and used them purely to check my progress along the seafront. I'd been going well for the last hour or two, let's hope I could keep it up.

I was on a stretch of flat promenade. There wasn't much to concentrate on, just put one foot in front of the other, and all the excitement of Weymouth and, eventually, Nothe Fort

---

[4] And I'm beginning to seriously question whether this does me more harm than good.

would soon be upon me. To pass the time, I fetched my phone from the zip pocket of my vest and called Eva.

We had a nice chat. I wanted to thank her for coming almost all the way to Kimmeridge, and to apologise for changing my mind. And I wanted to let her know that all was good, I was going to carry on at Weymouth, and I had this one in the bag. There – I'd said it now. No 'Spoons[5] for me tonight.

The times on this detailed version of my timing chart came at intervals of less than 10 minutes, and I kept knocking down the time on each spot as I passed entrances to car parks, bowling greens and the pier bandstand that were all marked on my list. It got busier once I got closer to town, but today wasn't a patch on the festivities and festival atmosphere of the previous year.

I rounded the corner onto Custom House Quay and suddenly, everything looked unfamiliar. Unlike the beach front, there were so many people everywhere here that I couldn't make out the pavement, the road or the front of the restaurants and bars. I couldn't even clearly see the bridge I knew I had to cross and was beginning to wonder if I'd taken a wrong turn. A check of my watch confirmed I was on the right route, so I just ran forward and had faith in the satellites and that once I'd weaved my way through the throng of people and avoided getting run over each time I dipped onto the road, I would eventually find myself at the steps up to Weymouth Bridge.

On the other side of the bridge, I passed one or two drinking establishments that I'd once frequented on hot summer days, crossed a little metal bridge covered in signs that admonished

---

[5] Spoons = Wetherspoons. A pub chain. But you knew that, right?

the owner of all responsibility for anything bad happening to anyone whilst anywhere near it, and made my way towards the checkpoint.

Last year, the route took me along the lower path that ran alongside the harbour below Nothe Gardens but this year the Climb South West sign attached to a pole was angled, seeming to point up the steps. I wasn't sure if this was a mistake – if the sign had maybe been knocked? – but, I was pretty sure that both routes took me to the checkpoint, so I opted for the one that matched the route I had on my watch and knew from 12 months prior that it took me to where I needed to be.

The path went on considerably longer than I remembered to the point where it crossed my mind that maybe Weymouth council had somehow removed a decades-old path just for giggles and I may have to turn around and go back to those steps after all. But then I spotted the old fashioned white and black Nothe Fort sign pointing up the slope to my right, and after a short climb under tree cover, I turned to the left and found myself at the entrance to the Fort at 7:25 pm, now a mere 30 minutes behind my 2023 time.

8

Saturday 22nd June 2024, 19:25

I headed through to the main area inside the fort knowing where to go and what to expect this year. I got a few greetings from people and offers of help from three Climb South West crew members to refill my bottles, get me a chair in the shade and to dig out my drop bag, but I was buzzing after pushing ahead on the times and declined all but the chair for now. I took my pack off and sat down just to rest for a minute and gather my thoughts.

It didn't take long for me to realised I didn't really have any sensible thoughts to gather and a few minutes later I had my drop bag next to me. My watch went on charge, my bottles were off in the hands of someone a bit handy with a water container and tearing off the tops of Tailwind sachets, and I had a coffee on the way.

I chatted with Justin, explaining that I had almost quit at Kimmeridge and was then going to call it a day here at Nothe Fort, but had a second wind over the last few miles and was thoroughly enjoying myself now. And a minute later, I had a hotdog and a coffee, so was enjoying myself even more!

Over the next 15 minutes I swapped my t-shirt for a fresh one and moved my main headtorch from my drop bag into my race vest. A pack of both paracetamol and Pro-Plus caffeine pills were stashed into an easy access pocket, and my MP3 went into the left front pocket ready to deploy once I got going. I dumped everything vaguely flapjack flavoured or shaped from my pack and replaced them with gels and chews as they had been working out much better over the last few hours. A few more packs of Tailwind into the bottom of the stretch pocket on the back of my vest, my watch back on my wrist at just over 90% battery – it hadn't really needed charging – and my drop-bag back with the others, and I was ready to go.

At ten minutes to 8 o'clock, Justin walked with me to the entrance, chatting away cheerfully and encouraging me on while giving me directions for the first chunk of the route towards the next checkpoint at Abbotsbury.

This was it. Despite being 99% committed to quitting at Kimmeridge... and then at Weymouth... I found myself continuing on in high spirits and with a real sense of excitement. I love the night sections of ultramarathons, and I was really looking forward to tonight, totally convinced that I'd sorted all my woes and now it was just a case of enjoying myself to the end.

I twiddled through Nothe Gardens and onto the roads of Rodwell, this section of the route having far more uphill than I remembered. I passed a few brightly coloured people running in the other direction who enthusiastically wished me luck, and as more runners passed by, I realised they were part of a running club. Then someone called my name and mentioned that they'd run this race – some of it with me – last year! My inability to recognise faces meant I had no real idea who it was, but it was amazing to bump into a group of random runners a good 40 miles from home and at least one of who knew me!

The runners (and the encouragement from them) faded as I crossed a new-looking metallic bridge that I vaguely remembered from the previous year. I was using the map on my watch a fair bit here. I knew how to get to Nothe Fort from the start with my eyes closed, and there wasn't much in the way of options once you got on the coast path the other side of the Portland Causeway, but the chunk in between was a few miles of road and tarmac trail with the odd turn here and there, and I wasn't confident enough to navigate without a little digital help.

I was still going uphill, and it was taking its toll on both my energy and my enthusiasm. Everything started feeling hard work again, and I was a bit concerned about that bloody timing chart. All was good for now, but I knew that the latter parts of that previous section to Weymouth had been awful last year, and so doing better this year didn't necessarily mean that I was actually doing *well* – just a bit less shit than last year. More worrying was that I remember the turbochargers kicking in last year just a few miles ahead of where I was now and having several hours of great progress. I was feeling far from convinced that the same would happen this year.

It was time to deploy the music. I only ever put one earphone in while running ultras so I can easily chat with people and hear the sounds around me and having lost the rubber cup on the right earphone during some race or other, I'd decided to chop it off before this one. It made sorting out the wire from the MP3 player so much easier, and after just a minute of fiddling without breaking stride, I had *The Phantom*

Buzz by Declan McKenna playing into my left ear. Not generally my first choice for music, but it was the start of the set that Oz, my son, had played the drums for in his first band – *Heads in the Door* – at the Anvil in Bournemouth last night. Hearing the first notes brought back the memories of him confidently playing on stage with his bandmates, putting on a great show, and I glowed a little with pride while making my way along the road.

I had expected the turn onto the Rodwell Trail to come much sooner than it did, so much so that I was considering turning back down the hill I'd just climbed thinking I'd cocked up. But there it was, the tiny stretch of road that took me from the pavement onto the tarmac path that ran along the route of the disused railway and took me all the way to the causeway road to Portland. The track was so flat it would be plain rude not to run, even though I didn't feel like it at all.

I had picked up a technique over the last few hours for handling the transition from walking to running, and it still seemed to be working. It involved leaning forward from my ankles and almost falling into a slow, shuffly run that initially seemed no faster than walking, mainly because it *was* no faster than walking. But it felt like no extra effort either and, over the course of the next 60 seconds, my feet naturally sped up until I was running at a slow but steady pace. It worked here again as it had before, and after 10 minutes of running I was in sight of the Weymouth end of the causeway road. On the final stretch to the road, I pulled out my timing chart and found that I was 29 minutes behind 2023. Somehow, amazingly, I was still going just a little faster than last year.

The traffic was constant in both directions along the road, so I was going to have to wait for the pedestrian crossing to do its thing and let me get safely to the other side. I pressed the button and resigned myself to a delay but quite unexpectedly, the lights changed immediately and I was soon on my way up into Wyke Regis, following the South West Coast Path diversion that took me on quite a long diversion around some steps that had collapsed a little over a year before.

The route went down a couple of narrow alleyways, then through a housing estate which ended up being a bit of a drag. From experience last year, I knew it would take a while, and it didn't disappoint. I'd been running with people and chatting away last year, but so far this time, I hadn't really had any company since Weymouth. I wasn't too bothered, though. I was just pushing on, concentrating on trying to keep ahead of those timing points.

As I went along the roads, I kept getting completely blinded by the low sun hitting my absolutely filthy glasses. Anyone who wears glasses will know that the technical fibres in running t-shirts and shorts do nothing but smear sweat and grease around the lenses, and as I knew I was passing by the edge of a hopefully busy camping field soon, I was readying myself to ask someone there for a tissue so I could get my vision back again!

"Go on Rich!" I heard someone call from the garden of a house on the other side of the road. I wasn't sure I'd heard right, but when they started clapping and seemed to be looking directly at me, I crossed over to say hello. I don't *think* I knew the person in the garden (apologies if I do!), and figured they were watching the tracker and catching people as they went by.

On the garden wall was a mini aid station, with jugs of water and a few bowls of sweets. I didn't fancy any sweets having just filled up back at the checkpoint, but grabbed a couple of cups of water, having a chat with the wonderful lady who'd put on this unexpected support for us runners!

"Do you need anything else?" she asked, and I had a sudden thought.

"You don't have a tissue handy, do you? My glasses are filthy so I keep getting blinded by the sun and this t-shirt is no good at cleaning them!"

"Of course, give me a moment," she said, rushing back into the house, and coming back 30 seconds later with a few tissues.

"Thank you so much – I'll be able to see again!" I said with delight and thanked her again for everything while heading on my way, a big smile on my face brought on by the kindness of strangers.

And the smile didn't fade as I realised I had now reached the final few houses and took the turn onto the path that led down past the campsite – where I now didn't need to bother anyone for a tissue as I passed – and back onto the proper South West Coast Path.

By the time I had finished the detour and was back on the path, the smile had faded somewhat. I was on a narrow, overgrown track where the surface once again slanted down at an annoying angle towards the water of the Fleet on my left. I tried to run, but struggled to keep my balance with each step, and found it easier to take up a fast walk. I was just beginning to get the hang of this when the path ahead disappeared underwater.

Well, this was new! I'd come along this path twice during races in the past, and there was no spot where it just ended! What the hell? I checked my watch, and I was apparently still on the right route. A moment of thought later, and it dawned on me.

There was a spot around here where the route followed the back of a little bay. I'd passed by in the dark during one race when the ground was very wet, and another time when the route was on firm, dry sand. I peered around the hedge to my right, and surmised that today, the tide was *all* the way in – there was no sand at all, and the water lapped at the back of the bay, leaving a narrow, muddy and very soggy bit of slightly raised ground that was the only possible option for me to take. I didn't know it at the time, but high tide here was 8:08pm, and it was just 25 minutes later when I was trying to figure out the confusion of a sudden and unexpected meeting with the sea.

I squelched onto the vegetation being splashed gently by the water, annoyed as the first step got my socks soaked through but glad that it was a warm summer evening and they would surely dry out quickly, even at night. I swore a few times as my feet submerged again, but it wasn't long before I was on firmer ground, still following around the back of the bay. I stepped over a final wet patch and, ignoring the steps that I'd used in the past which were further around the water, I cut through a gap in the bushes onto a dry track and up onto firm ground that took me in the right direction. I had a momentary rush of relief having got through that section without getting lost or completely ruining my feet, and then got on with the job at hand – following the path round to the right and onwards to the military camp that I knew I would be passing soon. The music in my ear switched over to *Gasoline* by I Prevail, a metalcore track of epic screamy-shoutiness! If this wasn't going to get me motivated, nothing would.

I stayed close to the water but on a bank high enough above to keep my feet dry and continued on the gently curving path, avoiding the tall grass that I had fought my way through last year. I was soon on the uphill road that would lead me back onto the narrow coast path the ran adjacent to the military. It was 8:43 pm, making me 27 minutes behind last year – still gaining, minute by minute… but now was crunch time. On the far side of the camp, in just a few minutes time, I'd reach the spot where the rocket boosters ignited in 2023, and I really didn't think I had the same kind of oomph available this year.

Reaching the far side and descending the gently sloping path, still all on my own, I picked up pace just a little in the hope that something magical might happen. It wasn't magical, but I was running, and I was running a little faster than I had been. Hopefully my memory of last year was over exaggerated, and even though I felt slower today I would soon find that I was actually making good progress.

I went through Littlesea Holiday Park, across green grass and past caravans, then back on narrow paths with the water of the Fleet gently wetting the shore next to my feet before coming to the almost 180-degree turn at Tidmoor. It took just under 20 minutes to get there, all the while I was running, walking and hoping that I was moving fast enough to keep pace with the 2023 time. At the turn, I was met with the disappointing news that I'd dropped back by 1 minute. Only a minute, but I'd been pushing much harder than I should have been, and far from being boosted by the fact that I was mere seconds away from last year's pace, my mind went into reverse and started losing all enthusiasm.

"Stop this!" I shouted out loud to myself, angrily. Every time I saw my pace slipping, my mood went downhill – it was getting bloody ridiculous. One minute, that was all. And it was probably a rounding error, in which case I was going at the same speed as last year, which was the best I was hoping for. And yet, my stupid, tired head was like Eeyore, down in the dumps again.

I was back in a military area, warnings not to touch anything metal dotted around, and signs to stick to the path periodically dotted around the path. Sunset was imminent, the air cool but not cold, certainly far more pleasant than the daytime. The only irritating thing was the sun being so low in the sky and with me heading west, it was permanently sat just below the cap of my hat, but if I pulled it any lower, I'd be blind to what was ahead, so I just had to put up with it.

I kept checking my watch to make sure I was on the route, even though there was no real need. My confidence was low, my energy lower, and despite trying to keep up a shuffling run, I was walking a lot more than I felt I should have been. The hard-baked mud was tough on my feet, threatening to twist ankles, and even when there was no camber it was uneven, and the lumps seemed to continuously hit painful spots on my feet. My toes were rubbing painfully in my shoes, still feeling damp from when they were partly submerged an hour or so ago.

The next timing point was about an hour on from the Tidmoor turn, so right now I had no real frame of reference for my pace. With that, I tried to take the optimistic view and managed to talk myself into believing that I was moving OK, as fast as last year. I told myself that when I finally go to Coastguard Road – where the checkpoint had been for the Oner a few years back, and the next point on my chart – I would be met with good news.

The sky darkened as the sun slipped below the horizon, the water of the Fleet shimmering away trapped behind the mound of pebbles that formed Chesil Beach to the south. Ahead of me, I spotted a couple of people in race kit and the desire to chase, to try and catch them up kicked in despite my tiredness. In a boost to my mood, I actually managed it, although I really felt like I was working far too hard to maintain the pace.

Having caught up with them, I chatted with Callum Parnell and Ollie Osborne as I passed, one of whom was stopped for a moment. After checking everything was OK, I continued onwards, and now I was the hare and had to keep up that pace that I'd been finding on the edge of sustainable. I pushed on, and was convinced I had built up a gap, but 5 minutes later when I glanced back expecting to see no one, I saw that Callum and Ollie were not far behind at all.

And oddly, I think that was it: the point of no return for my head.

9

The quiet sounds of nature

Saturday 22nd June 2024, 21:43

There was no doubt about it, I was definitely slowing down. I don't know if it was my brain giving up, or the rest of my body having reached the end of what it was capable of today, but everything started to become exponentially harder work. I kept pushing on, making my way across the grass as the light continued to drop, ushering in the darkness of the night.

I didn't have my head torch on yet as I could still see ahead, but it was getting close to needing it as the ground was blending into one dark green mass and I didn't want to twist my ankle in a dip, crack or hole that I didn't spot in the dark.

I walked past a big building surrounded with a high brick wall, and finally figured that this must be Moonfleet Manor, a name I'd heard before, and spotted several times on the map – it's always nice to put a face to the name, so to speak. I turned right immediately as the wall ended because it felt like the right thing to do, but a quick check of my watch showed it certainly wasn't, so I backtracked and continued in the direction I had been going before my random turn.

The path headed inland, away from the water and the soft, flattened grass extending out in front of a low stone wall to my right looked so incredibly comfortable. I wanted a break from the effort, from the fight inside my head. Just for minute. So, I dropped my poles and sat myself down on the ground, taking a few deep breaths and admiring the colour of the post-dusk sky, the beautiful view and the quiet sounds of nature in the late evening.

Callum and Ollie caught up and passed by checking I was OK, and I explained I was just resting for a moment. In the minute or so since sitting down, though, an overwhelming tiredness had risen in me, and when the two headtorches were almost out of sight, I lay down on my side on the grass, closed my eyes and wished for sleep. I didn't set an alarm, I didn't care if I slept for 2 minutes or 2 hours, it just didn't matter to me right now. It felt like a last-ditch attempt at trying to turn around my loss of motivation and find some energy for the race.

Seven minutes after stopping, I was dragging myself up off the ground. As always happened, the grass had lost the comfy floaty-soft bed feel it offered when I had laid down and become scratchy, itchy, and buzzing with insects, most of which had probably just bitten me[6]! Did I feel better? No, not at all, but I was ready to get going and I knew that a rest often started bringing benefits some 10 or 20 minutes after you get moving. Fingers crossed then.

I got walking, slowly, and while starting off I cracked out a couple of Pro Plus caffeine pills from the front of my vest and downed them with some drink. Hopefully another burst of caffeine would help.

---

[6] Absolutely right – I had 7 massive bites in a row behind my right knee which itched like absolute demons for about 10 days after the race!

Those 7 minutes had turned the evening from light enough to get by without a headtorch, to definitely needing one, so I strapped my headtorch on and clicked through the 3 brightness levels on the 2 different spreads of light. I chose the lowest brightness but the widest beam, bringing some detail to the view in front.

The next timing point on my chart was Coastguard Road, and I was pretty sure I'd already passed it. After all, it was almost quarter past 10, so I'd be really, really late if…

Hang on.

I recognise that gate.

And sure enough, here was the end of Coastguard Road. I checked my watch and waited for my brain to do some basic subtraction. I was now 43 minutes behind last year. I'd lost 15 minutes over the last hour. At the time, it didn't occur to me that I'd been stopped for 7 minutes. Instead, it just served to confirm what I already knew – I was switching off, mentally and physically, and my race was done.

Across the road, I started into a field which brought with it a new problem for me: moths. At least I think they were moths. Hundreds and hundreds of them, flying into the light, banging into my face, up my nose, in my mouth. I tried to sweep them away, but more just came. It wasn't a swarm so much as a light cloud, but the ones that kept trying to get into my lungs were the most annoying, making me cough and splutter as I walked along.

Thankfully, just at the point where I was thinking maybe I should just walk in the dark, the crops in the field changed and the moths subsided. As I'm writing this, I've just realised that I could have carried my torch for a moment – that would at least have kept them away from my face. Something to keep in mind if it happens again.

I turned onto a tree-covered path which felt very dark and a bit spooky, freaking me out a little. It's not something that normally happens to me during races, but I kept looking behind, my frazzled mind playing tricks on me and making me think I was hearing twigs crack.

At least the fear of Freddy Kruger coming up behind sped me up a bit, although I remembered this whole tree-tunnel section being short before a turn to the left, but someone had just about tripled the length today. My watch eventually showed the bend over to the left and I headed out from under the tree cover and towards a gate ahead.

There were still hints of light in the sky and while my headtorch was helping show up things directly in front, the periphery was dark. I almost went all the way over to an obvious metal gate before I had a pang of déjà vu. In the middle of an icy night in April, I'd found that the coast path route wasn't through this gate, but instead over a stile situated a little way along the fence to my left, so I turned my head and the torch light flooded the area, revealing the step over the fence.

It wasn't far to the stile, but the grass was long and by the time I got to the wooden structure, my lower legs and feet were damp. The moisture in the air was condensing on the tiny cooler blades of grass, and my feet were knocking all the droplets off onto my shoes which found their way through to my socks.

The next couple of fields were quite long but thankfully had short grass so my feet didn't get any wetter. I could see the swinging beams of headtorches far in the distance, and as I headed straight towards them, the lights turned to the right and started heading uphill.

By the time I reached the bottom of the hill, I was in quite a bit of discomfort. A blister on my left heel had decided to kick up a stink in the last 10 minutes, and both my outer little toes felt rubbed raw, which wasn't unusual for me as I have wide feet but wasn't all that pleasant either.

Since the desire to push on and finish the race had waned to the point of no return, the niggles had surfaced. It was like it took quite a bit of mental effort to ignore them, and I didn't have much of that left at all. My legs ached, my pace was pathetically slow, and now my feet really bloody hurt.

"I'm stopping at Abbotsbury," I thought to myself, calculating that it wouldn't be more than a mile or two away.

"Why not West Bay? It's flat along that stretch," replied my brain, in an unusual moment of positivity.

"Forgotten about the shingle, dickhead? No, Abbotsbury. End of."

The argument was short lived, and I won.

I started up the hill. It wasn't much of a hill in real terms, and it wasn't very steep, so all that happened is I slowed down a bit more. The grasses were taller here, and the ground was surprisingly wet in patches, so I was having to weave around muddy puddles in an attempt to keep my feet dry.

I stopped for a second and looked back the way I'd just come and was surprised to see 4 separate head torches casting swinging beams across the long field below. I figured one must be Jay, but I couldn't work out how 3 people had joined up with him – I didn't think there were that many people in a group at this point in the race.

I was slowly continuing up the hill, music quietly playing in my ear, when I became aware of a rustling behind me. The jitteriness that I'd had back in that tree tunnel had long passed so I wasn't nervous, I just wondered what it was – a fox? A badger? A deer? I turned around and was surprised to see a dark figure running up the hill, his headtorch off. It was unusual not only as he almost completely blended in with the surroundings, but also because he was *running* up the hill. How the hell did anyone have the energy to be running uphill at this point? Then it twigged – he was running because he was in the early stages of a different race! The 100km runners started at Nothe Fort at 9pm, about 1 hour and 45 minutes earlier.

James Long was in the lead, and we exchanged a few cheerful words as he passed by. He cheekily said he was keeping his headtorch off so the people behind didn't know where he was.

"Well, it's a race, isn't it?" he added with a chuckle, as he disappeared off up the hill.

A few minutes later, while I was *still* going up this quite small hill, another guy passed me. His approach was much more obvious from the bright light of his headtorch, and I congratulated him on his progress.

"Well done, you're only a couple of minutes behind the leader," I said, trying to be helpful and encouraging.

"Ha ha! You mean I *am* the leader," he said with a laugh, which confused me for a bit. A minute after he'd gone, I remembered that the guy in the lead had kept his headtorch off, so the second place running genuinely thought he was in the lead. Cheeky!

It could have been annoying, having to keep stepping in to let people pass by, but I didn't mind as I was going so slowly and just starting to enjoy what was absolutely, definitely and without a shadow of a doubt the last few miles of my race. My mind was set, and I just had to plod through the final death throes of my 2024 Jurassic Coast 100 race.

The playlist of Oz's live songs from the previous night ended, and I swapped over to Bring Me the Horizon's *POST HUMAN: NeX GEn* album. It had been released the previous month, and I had listened to it whilst on holiday in Jersey, just enough to get familiar with a few songs, and then stashed it away to enjoy during this race. Sadly, I wasn't going to get to listen to much of it before I stopped.

I reached the top of the hill and knew where I was going for the next stretch, although even if I didn't it would have been obvious due to the steady stream of headtorches passing me and leading the way. Around the edge of a field and down a hill that I just about managed to build up pace to a jog towards the end. Across a road and through another bumpy, soft field during which the part of my brain that didn't want to quit made me swallow two salt pills, an energy gel and a whole load of water in the hope that some miracle might transform give me just enough of a boost over the next few minutes to continue. Then it was onto the start of the bigger hill – the last one before Abbotsbury.

I did a quick check of my timing chart, more just to make sure I hadn't suddenly and unexpectedly gained a load of time rather than because I cared about the actual time. Fifty-two minutes behind now.

The hill, which was about twice the height and length of the previous one, took bloody ages to climb. It was massively overgrown in sections, and in one particular corner I had to just trust that my watch was telling me the right way as I pushed through a wall of vegetation to find a secret portal housing a stile which took me through to the next field.

After a barrage of 100km runners passed by, their combined torchlight turning night into day, I reached a stone stile at the top of the hill and made my way across the short patch of grass to another wooden stile. It would have got very dark here had it been evening, as there was thick tree cover above for a few hundred metres. But at almost 11 pm, it was already dark and the only change I noticed was the tall tree trunks either side of me as I walked along the flat stretch, waiting for my breathing and heartrate to return to something like normal. It shouldn't really have been abnormal considering how slowly I'd climbed the hill, but it was another indication that my physiological state today was far from ideal.

The next few minutes were flat and quiet, the lights ahead disappearing into the distance, and the ones behind yet to catch me. I was caught and overtaken just before a spot I'd been confused at in the past, and I called to the runner who had made the same mistake as I had by taking the obvious looking track to the left.

"Straight ahead," I called out, and he came back up the hill, looking confused. "Just up that little hill," I explained, pointing directly ahead. "It's not very obvious." I caught him up, and we both trudged up the small hill and along the side of a very soft, freshly ploughed patch of land.

I'd passed along here twice previously, and it has been firm, solid ground covered in short grass, an ideal terrain to walk or run along. Today, however, not only was it hard work in the very soft mud, but it felt like we might be traipsing all over someone's crops, even along the edge. The two of us had seemed to have the same though, and we stopped and looked around to check the route, spotting a wooden stile to the side just behind us. A quick check of the wooden post attached showed a South West Coast Path acorn symbol, so across we went. This was a new path for me which, judging by the acorn, is the correct route and one I've mistakenly missed in the past.

What an absolute bugger it was too! It was ridiculously overgrown – the worst section of the whole race so far. Tall plants of all the spiky varieties pushed their way onto the path, and as I made my way along I had to push aside gorse, stinging nettles, brambles, and thistles while more of those bloody moths fluttered in my face. The path ran parallel to the ploughed field, the fence tantalisingly close with the soft but flat and clear path the other side mocking me.

As annoying as the passage was, it was also strangely fun. It's not every day you get to go along an overgrown path in the middle of the night, regularly squashing into something spiky and stingy to let the faster runners behind pass by. There was no running going on for me, though. In fact, with all the stopping and the fight through the vegetation, combined with the slow climb a few minutes before, my watch cheerfully beeped a 28-minute mile at me.

It took me 17 minutes to cover the 1,000 metres of overgrown path, and when I escaped into the freedom of the wide-open space at 11:34pm, I was well and truly spent. At this pace, it would take me something like 5 hours to get to West Bay, and I didn't have the mental strength to put up with such a slow trudge. All I wanted to do was stop and fall asleep.

There wasn't far left to go though, just a winding descent along the ridge tops. My legs didn't like it though, quads shaking on the descent, and I was very thankful I had my poles to keep me upright. After crossing two stone stiles that I didn't remember ever meeting before and pulling in a couple more times to let people pass, I was out on the road – the final stretch to the checkpoint.

The road felt alien in the dark but with a mix of very slow running and walking I reached the car park entrance and approached the table. It was 11:40pm, I'd climbed just over 8,500 feet over 57.4 miles of the Jurassic Coast 105 race… and I was done.

10

Saturday 22nd June 2024, 23:40

There was a bit of a queue of people at the table, the big clump of 100km runners that had passed me refilling fluids and grabbing snacks. I stood a bit back from the table, stretching my legs and, quite frankly, revelling in the thought of not having to run any more.

When the group at the table thinned, I ambled over. I was a bit nervous. I'd DNF'd two ultras in the past, albeit one of them (the Arc of Attrition) I DNF'd 3 times! Only one of those times, all the way back in 2018, had I quit without some kind of genuine injury or medical issue. And so, today, I was going to bring my ultra DNF tally up to 5.

There's a saying that goes something like "if you're guaranteed to finish, you're not aiming high enough", and I wondered if that applied here. When I set out this morning, I knew the race was going to be hard work, but I hadn't really contemplated *not* finishing. I'd had most of the day to come to terms with it though, having aborted two attempts to quit earlier. I felt like I'd given it a good bash.

Lou, who'd made me that lovely cheese and ham sandwich back at Lulworth, was behind the table in charge of everything

84

at the checkpoint, so I told her my news. Maybe there was something in my eyes or the way I said it, but I got no argument from Lou, and I was thankful. I didn't want to have to fight to end my race – I wasn't sure I had the energy.

"I'm not quite sure what's going on but have a seat for now and we'll sort something out," said Lou with a smile, as she bustled around sorting things out for the checkpoint.

There was a chap in the only chair available, and I didn't really think I deserved a chair as I didn't need to rest my legs for an onward journey, so I just sat down on the dusty gravel floor of the car park and got chatting with Chris Richards. He was the guy in the chair, and he was pretty much mummifying his bare feet in tape and what looked like gauze pads. He told me that they had ended up really sore since he'd started the 100km race just under 14 miles ago back at Nothe Fort, and this was a belt-and-braces approach he hoped would get him to the end.

Chris didn't seem to be in much of a rush, and we chatted for a bit more before he got himself up and I helped him sort his funky arrangement of battery and at least 2 lights attached to a couple of straps that wrapped around his pack. With a red light flashing on his back and bright light shining from his chest, Chris headed off towards West Bay.

A while later I met Lou's husband Rob as I sat on the step at the side door of their van, behind the checkpoint desk. I was getting quite cold so had put on my emergency thermal top and my waterproof coat, both mandatory kit and right now – even in June – very welcome!

Lou and Rob were lovely, we had a great chat and they were really happy and friendly to me and all the racers that came through. At least one 100-mile racer came through – Jack Crossley – and I had a slight pang of both enviousness at his continued journey, and disappointment that I had finished. But a quick reminder to myself of what was to come, and how I'd felt over the last hour or two, had me convinced I'd made the right decision.

The plan had been that I wait for the sweeper bus which would be past when the checkpoint closed, but a volunteer called Ben was calling it a night at what I would guess was sometime around 12:30am, and as he lived near West Bay, he offered to give me a lift there. Not only was the next checkpoint in a building and so would be considerably warmer than sat outside, but there was also a bigger selection of food there, and I was beginning to get very hungry, especially for something other than gels or chews.

Ben drove for 20 minutes or so with his stinky, tired passenger and dropped me off at the Salt House in West Bay, coming in to let the checkpoint manager know who I was and why I'd arrived on wheels instead of by foot. Sometime around 1am, I took up a seat at the back of the hall, all set to wait for a while.

My plan was to get to Lyme Regis – as that was where my drop bag was – and then get Eva to come out and pick me up from there at a more sensible time in the morning. I'd messaged her but, like any sensible person, she was asleep. I'd also messaged my sister Niki, but she's not sensible so she replied, and we had a little chat by text.

The checkpoint had music, and it had pork pies, but it didn't have a huge amount of warmth. The stone building of the Salt House was pretty cold, especially with the door open, but I wasn't shivering, so it was an improvement on my situation back at Abbotsbury. And I had a cup of tea too. All in all, it was a much nicer experience than trudging along shingle… although, that *is* what I'd signed up for, and I kept getting little moments of sadness at missing the experience as I thought of tough bits, the beautiful bits, the horrible bits… and the finish in Exmouth, something I wouldn't get to do today.

A steady flow of people came through, and I hadn't been in the building long before someone came over to me tentatively, checking he'd recognised me correctly. It was Darren Curtis-White, the chap I'd grabbed the Calippo with back at Ringstead last year. He'd had a bit of a disaster just a few miles from the end of the 105-mile race last year, so was back this year doing the 100km, and was having a tremendous time by the sounds of it. He was all laughter and smiles and looked like he was having a lot of fun.

A little later, I found myself chatting to Matt Dalton as he passed through a bit after 1:30am. I say *passed through*, but it was more like he'd taken up residence! Even though he was absolutely knackered, he didn't stop smiling. Except, that is, when he was asleep on the floor for 20 minutes, his legs raised up on a chair. There's definitely something magical and motivating about a happy demeanour, and Matt had that in spades. I'm usually pretty cheerful, but I had just felt too knackered to do much smiling during the race this time round.

I figured I'd have to wait here for the sweeper bus until the checkpoint closed at 5am but, with the Abbotsbury checkpoint now closed, Lou and Rob appeared in the door to say hello to the checkpoint crew. They were on their way to Lyme Regis to start helping out there and offered me a lift in their van.

And so, at about 2:45am, we headed over to Lyme, a hilly but quiet drive, where we spent the whole time chatting about races and our funny (and sometimes scary) experiences. Rob falling asleep in the middle of a road was one particular scary story – definitely not ideal!

Apart from being absolutely exhausted, I felt generally OK. Nothing was broken, the foot blisters had been the most annoying thing and even those had calmed down. My legs ached a bit, but nothing compared to if I'd done the rest of the race. It seems that the second half is where all the aches and pains that follow you around for the week afterwards come from.

Rob parked up in the big Lyme Regis car park next to the football club which served as the checkpoint, and we walked the short distance over to the building. I was in a daze and thankful that Lou explained the situation to whoever was in charge. I was sent in to find a seat, and ensconced myself at the back of the room, sticking my pack on the floor and taking up residence on a comfortable chair.

I was offered food and opted for beans on toast with a cheeky fried egg on top, and a few minutes later I had wolfed it down. Sometimes, the simplest food can feel like heaven, and this was one of those times! Afterwards, I wandered off to the other end of the building to get my drop bag, which was one of the two reasons I'd come to Lyme.

The second reason was to see Bea Griffiths, a good friend and great runner who I didn't get to see nearly often enough! She was also a chef, and today, was running the kitchen, which is why my egg-topped beans on toast had been just spot on!

Bea came out the kitchen when the rush died down and we chatted for a while about training, races and our common friends. On the subject of races, Bea is taking part in the Tor des Géants in September, an absolutely epic 330km race through the Vale D'Aosta in Italy with just under *80,000 feet* of climb! And on the subject of common friends, Darren came in a bit after half past three, still laughing, joking and looking like he was enjoying himself after six and a half hours and just about halfway through his 100km race.

The exhaustion of the day, the night and the previous week became an overwhelming weight, and I lay down on the floor in a little spot between the table and the wall, hoping I wouldn't get in anyone's way. It didn't feel like I had any sleep, but I *did* feel like I woke up, and there was a crusty spot down my cheek where I'd obviously dribbled while snoozing – very elegant! I could hear a familiar voice at the table above me. It was nearly 6am, and Matt Dalton was in the house, still cheerful, still swearing, and looking even more knackered than he had back at West Bay!

I must have spent four or five hours at Lyme, but when I think back, it felt like minutes. When you're mentally exhausted, it gets difficult to separate events after the fact, and my memory of the whole time is just a blur.

I remember saying bye to Matt as he headed off to Beer, marvelling (and jealous) of the fact he'd already had one or two ciders enroute!

And I had an absolutely bloody delicious bacon sandwich, courtesy of Bea.

I remember being sat opposite Chris Richards at the table, talking him through the next section. He was having a hard time, and I gave him one of my spare laminated timing charts[7] so he could keep an eye on the cutoffs.

Outside the windows, there were people – excited and nervous, fresh and ready. I thought they might be here for football – after all, it was Sunday morning and we were in a football club building. After a while, my brain twigged that they were here for the 50km race, running from here to Exmouth and setting off at 8am. An easy 31 miles? Don't you believe it! There's a *lot* of elevation *and* the Undercliff between here and Exmouth – there was nothing easy about this 50km!

At about 7:30am, it felt like time to get going. I'd sent some messages to Eva and was waiting for her to wake up and find out what time she could get over to pick me up. But more importantly, my Google investigations while sat in the checkpoint had suggested that on this Sunday morning, the Cornish Bakery in town opened at 8am, the Tesco Express across the road from it was already open, and I was hoping they'd been baking chocolate croissants!

I'd also had a realisation that didn't fill me with joy – I had to do my steps.

What are you talking about? you might think. Well, for the previous 2,127 days, I'd covered at least 7,500 steps each day and unfortunately, as I'd stopped the race just before midnight, I'd covered less than 1,000 as I sat in the Lyme Regis Football Club. I had work to do.

I left the building at about 7:40am, in time to walk down towards the car park and bump into Chris, who'd also just left,

---

[7] Of course I had spares! One set in my pack, and one set in my drop bag. Just in case I lost one. Or two.

and send him in the right direction – across the car park and down the steps to the seafront. I, on the other hand, went the shorter and easier route down the road into town. A croissant, Cornish Pasty and coffee awaited me.

It took a while to get down to the bottom of the hill and then back up the other side to the shops – why did everything around here have to be so bloody hilly?! But sometime after 8am, I was sat on a bench above the end of Marine Parade, watching the 50km runners passing by below. I wanted to shout encouragement down, but a couple of things stopped me. First, it was a little after 8am on a Sunday morning, and some idiot yelling from a bench was probably not what the residents of Lyme wanted to hear. And secondly, I had a face full of hot and delicious Cornish Pasty with a chocolate croissant and a steaming black Americano balanced on the slats of the bench next to me.

While sat on the bench, I received a message from Eva:

Morning. Glad you're ok. So where are you? Lyme Regis? We had all planned to leave at 9:30 is that ok? I'll see if I can get them moving earlier but it might be tricky x

Teenagers. Good luck with that! I replied with:

Yeah, that's fine! I've got a pasty and a chocolate croissant and a coffee and I'm sat looking at the sea now. May see if the hotel bar is open that I just passed…

And I meant it. A pint would go down so well!

After I'd finished my pasty and chocolate croissant, I took a look at my watch and resigned myself for another bit of walking. I set off, ostensibly under the guise of getting more steps, but I was also on a side-quest to see if I could find a drinking establishment that was open a little after 8 o'clock on a Sunday morning. Sadly, it was not to be – the pub up the top of the hill was dead to the world, and the hotel whose doors stood open housed a shiny bar but also a slightly confused lady who told me that the bar didn't open until much, much later. This wasn't Bideford, after all.

The step count was still disappointingly low on my watch face, but I had an idea and turned onto the sea front, heading towards the car park that was home to an innocuous set of steps which would have taken me up to a fascinating and tough stretch of coast path – the Lyme to Seaton Undercliff.

For some reason I had a desire to see those. I've no idea why, it just felt like if I got to see the continuation of the race route out of Lyme Regis, I could rest a little easier, like I hadn't missed out on *all* of the later bits. And so, halfway across an empty car park, once I could clearly see the staircase that led into the trees which filled the entire view west, I turned around to head back through the town to the car park next to the checkpoint where I was going to be picked up.

It was a lot busier on the way back. There were a lot of runners that passed by and I kept an eye out in case they were part of the Jurassic Coast races, but none that passed had numbers on. I said good morning in any case, getting about a 50% success rate on return greetings. After I'd passed the famous brightly coloured beach huts on the front at Lyme Regis, I saw a couple more runners coming towards me, and eventually my shitty eyes resolved Bea and Anna. Bea had mentioned she was supposed to do 17 miles today as part of her Tor des Géants training, and here she was heading off towards the Undercliff, a particular delight (read: horror!) of the Jurassic Coast race. On the one occasion I've run it on relatively fresh legs, it was actually really good fun… but I had slept the night before, unlike Bea!

I was watching the approach of my family on Life360, and so it wasn't exactly a surprise when Ryan – my daughter's boyfriend – drove into the car park in his grey Ford Focus. Eva, Sophie and Oz were in the car, and as I clambered into the back, my watch buzzed to say I'd hit my 7,500-step goal, which was a relief.

We drove back via West Bay, something that had been promised to the other occupants of the car, and initially to me had seemed like an unwanted detour. I wanted to get home and get some sleep, but they'd come all the way out here to pick me up, so I kept my mouth shut.

Sat on the pebbles with most of my family and yet another pasty – this time a Beef and Stilton one – and having had possibly the best ice cream I've ever eaten I was delighted that we'd stopped here. That ice cream was a couple of scoops of some delicious ice cream, the flavour of which I can't remember, in a cone… *topped with Mr Whippy!* I'm a sucker for vanilla, so Mr Whippy ice cream hits the spot, but always feel like I've missed out on the flavoured stuff. This absolute beauty combined the two!

And then I was home.

And I slept for 90 minutes.
And somehow survived the rest of Sunday.

11

I was happy

At home

When I got home, I was still happy I'd quit. It was the right decision.

I was happy with my decision when I woke up after a nap, early evening on Sunday.

For the whole of Monday, I was in a daze. Luckily, I'd had the foresight to book the day off work. And I was still happy I'd finished when I had.

12

It was never about the time

Tuesday 25th June 2024

On Tuesday, I wish I had a bit of Matt Dalton's spirit. During the race, he was knackered. No, scratch that... he was absolutely fucked! And that was at West Bay, not much over half of the way to the finish.

And yet, he wore a smile on his face, made jokes, and staggered out of the building to finish in just over 31 hours.

But to him, the time didn't matter. The important thing was that he was on an *adventure*. Getting to Exmouth and having fun along the way was the goal, not to finish in some arbitrary time.

And as my tiredness dissipated over the following days, I got more and more pissed off that I'd missed the whole point of the race.

It was never about the time.

13

I do think there was something wrong with me that day. I don't know exactly what, but I have a few theories.

First, my training had been off since the end of the previous year, maybe around the time I started a new job. Going from "your time is your own" for 12 years to being under someone else's schedule definitely has a bit of an impact. When working for myself, I tended to run to work more (as I didn't care what I smelt like!), train at random times of day when I felt like it, and even catch some sleep in my office if I'd overdone it with too much running or too many late nights.

I hadn't *enjoyed* many runs over the 6 months before the race, either. They mostly felt like hard work, very few had even the slightest hint of enjoyment. My Garmin watch was doing all it could to tell me something was up too: resting heart rate jumped by 10bpm, HRV was through the floor, Body Battery was... well... flat[8].

And to top it off, for the week before the race, everyone in the house was coughing and sneezing. I was determined to avoid whatever lurgy they had (mainly through the clinically proven method of "hoping I didn't catch it", plus the odd

---

[8] Most of that sorted out over the 3 months after the race, so there was definitely some new (to me at least) long-running health issue that seemed to linger for 6 months or so.

vitamin C tablet when I remembered), but while I was pressing the shutter button on the camera during the gig on the Friday evening before the race, I was also trying to rid myself of an irritating cough that had been bothering me for the past 48 hours.

But, on the whole and with a couple of weeks to think about it, I think the cause of my DNF was that I was focusing on the wrong thing.

I went into the race assuming I'd finish. I made a timing chart with several columns all the way down to just making the cutoffs, but despite all those extra columns, only one mattered to me – the optimistic one. The one that I felt like I *should* have been able to achieve. And when the chance of doing that disappeared, I fell apart. I wasn't interested in "just finishing", although I didn't realise that at the time.

DNFs aren't all bad. This one, for instance, is great… *now!* It's taught me 2 very important lessons.

The first is that you have to train for these events and that training balances with the rest of your life. Be realistic, and if your whole life situation changes (i.e. a new job), then give yourself a bit of time to adapt.

And the second is more important… I'm getting scarily close to 50. I can't expect to keep improving my time for races, and if that's all that motivates me – all that *matters* – then I'm doomed.

Matt didn't care about the time he finished in.

He didn't have laminated timing charts that took hours and hours to prepare.

And Matt wasn't in the minority... *I* was the weirdo, obsessed with the plastic numbers hiding in my race vest.

I've entered the Devon Coast to Coast for 2025 – the only "long" Climb South West event that I haven't done. There are differing answers to the question of how long it is, but somewhere within a few miles of 115 seems about right.

It's not on the coast path, so part of me is a bit scared of the unknown, but a much bigger part of me is really excited for something new and different.

And, while I sit and write this just under 3 weeks after the Jurassic Coast race, I've decided to do the North Coast 110 again (and I'll be re-reading my book *Buckle Down* to remind myself what the hell I'm letting myself in for!). I have to get this monkey off my back, and what better way than 110 miles of lumps and bumps!

With 3 months until that race, I'm planning and training better. I had a week off after the Jurassic Coast race, but am now working on my diet, going to the gym a few times a week (which I've never done before, at least while running at the same time), and have something vaguely resembling a training plan.

But there'll be one very big difference with this race – I'm going to try my very best to make it about the *adventure*. Screw the finish time – that's not important.

There will be NO timing charts for this one!

If I train well and end up fit going in, then maybe the numbers will be suitably pleasing, but if not, who cares? I can barely remember the finish times of previous races, but I can tell you all about how I felt – happy and sad, energetic and exhausted, tired and buzzing, chatty or solitary. I can tell you what I saw – the views, the hills, the mud, the sunsets and sunrises, the hailstones and snow, the monuments, statues and obelisks, the waves crashing against the shores and the wind whipping my jacket.

All I have to do is get out there and fucking enjoy myself! Races like the Jurassic Coast 100 don't come cheap, so even when I'm absolutely ruined in the middle of it, I just need to take the next step.

I've written this before, and for some stupid reason I need to keep reminding myself, but here was my advice before my final (and successful) attempt at the Arc of Attrition:

I can stop when:
 (a) I get to the end,
 (b) I get timed out, or
 (c) I die.

So, there's 2 rules I need to add going into the next race:

Rule 1:
*There is **no** excuse not to finish.*

Rule 2:
Screw the finish time… Just have fun!

Let's see if I can stick to my new rules in October!

14

I mention several people during this book, and it would be remiss not to give an update on how it went for them.

There were 16 finishers in the 105-mile race from 31 starters.

The race was won by Justin Montague in an amazing 22:08:06!

Matt Dalton finished in 8th place with a time of 31:16:43, and Jay King came in 13th with a time of 34:37:47.

Sadly, Alex Loach, who had cheered me up as I ran with him into Kimmeridge, got as far as Lyme Regis in just under 22 hours, but no further. He had been through Abbotsbury almost an hour and a half before I turned in my tracker there.

In the 100km race, there were 54 starters, and 48 finishers, and James Long – the dark figure with his headtorch off who'd passed me on the hill before Abbotsbury – took the win in 12:48:30.

Darren Curtis-White finished in 9th place with a time of 14:42:44, and Chris Richards got all the way to the end in 23:08:53, despite his smashed-up feet just over 10 miles in, where I'd been chatting to him at Abbotsbury.

THE END

Before you go…

I genuinely hope you've enjoyed this book. If you did and have a few minutes to spare, I would be so grateful if you could leave a review (hopefully positive!) on Amazon, and maybe rave about how amazing it was to spend a few hours getting lost in these pages to all your friends on social media!

You can stay in touch over at:

www.swcpplod.co.uk

and if you've got any questions or feedback, you can use the contact form or social media links on the site.

Thanks again for taking the time to read my book!

Printed in Dunstable, United Kingdom